YOU MAKE THE DIFFERENCE

THROUGH
ENJOYABLE
&
EFFECTIVE MEETINGS

Kay Kay

In collaboration with Tim Kay

You Make the Difference
www.youmakethedifference.net

Second Edition
First Edition published in 2012

Book designed and published by Tim Kay
University of Life

www.unioflife.net

You Make the Difference logo
& flip chart illustrations © Tim Kay
All other illustrations and images © Microsoft Corporation

Author photo by Lina&Linda AB
Stockholm, Sweden

DEDICATION

This book is dedicated to those people who, through their commitment to making some difference in the world, continue to turn up and participate in meetings that are less enjoyable and effective than they would wish, and to all those admirable meeting managers who endeavor to make their meetings as enjoyable and effective as possible.

CONTENTS

ACKNOWLEDGMENTS

I am grateful to Tim Kay for the quality of his design and production of this book and to Jane Cotton for her insightful and meticulous editing. I value their commitment, encouragement and generous support.

I appreciate all of those participants of so many meetings, whose willingness, trust and openness resulted in so much mutual learning and development.

The thoughts, insights, suggestions, methods, procedures and processes in this book have been developed over several decades. I am indebted to those people who have generously shared their methods, techniques and processes through meetings, workshops, training programs, conferences and networking. However, due to the ways in which many of these methods have been adopted and adapted by many people over time it is difficult to identify the originators. Consequently I must acknowledge in a broader way then I would wish the creativity of many inspirational people.

I am grateful to my friends and colleagues in the Findhorn Community for their commitment to group decision making and bringing forth the wisdom in groups. Especially to Jane Hera, www.marvellousmeetings.co.uk who taught me so much through her approaches to creating inclusive and enjoyable meetings. From my time in the Antipodes I am indebted to friends in the Australasian Facilitators Network who have done so much to raise the bar on the quality of facilitation and from whom I have learned a great deal.

I appreciate these people, along with many others, who make significant contributions to the meetings, events, conversations and decisions that are so vitally important for the empowerment of individuals, the transition of our towns, the evolving of our societies and the sustainability of our world.

KAY KAY

1

UNDERSTANDING MEETINGS

What are your attitudes towards meetings? Do you enjoy them or does your heart sink at the thought of attending them? If you manage meetings, is this your choice? Do you relish the role? Is this something you do because someone has to do it? Or is it a role you feel obliged to carry out that you approach with gloom or even dread?

Contrasting experiences

The first meetings that I attended as a young woman were mind numbingly tedious. They were frustrating, disempowering, unnecessarily lengthy and often excruciatingly embarrassing due to the clashing egos of the people involved. It was only my passion and commitment to the project that kept me turning up to these dreadful events until the project was completed. It was many years before I was once again willing to risk subjecting myself to such an unpleasant experience!

When my passion and commitment to another project eventually overcame my reluctance to attend meetings, I received a very pleasant surprise. These meetings were skillfully managed, inclusive, efficient, productive and thoroughly enjoyable.

These two contrasting experiences made me realize that there are skills involved in the management of meetings that, when employed, make the difference between an effective and an ineffective meeting and an enjoyable or an uncomfortable experience.

The intention for this book is to share the information and experience gained during 5 decades of participation in and the management of meetings. To help to make meeting participation and management easy, enjoyable and effective for all those involved.

A growing need

The need for meetings appears to be growing. Most of us are now likely to attend more meetings at work, as part of our family responsibilities and in our leisure or volunteer activities than ever before. Many of us, who have not previously been involved with meetings, may now be required to attend them.

As engagement in community projects, activities and movements increases, people who may never have previously attended meetings, might now choose do so. For people to remain involved and engaged and to believe that they can make a meaningful contribution to their society, these meetings will need to be effective, productive and enjoyable.

People's attitudes towards these meetings can vary from positive enthusiasm to dread and avoidance, with most people somewhere in between. These attitudes often result from previous experiences of meetings and of the quality and effectiveness of those events. If people have found the meetings they have attended to be dry, uninteresting, frustrating or disempowering they are not likely to want to participate in future meetings.

Meeting the future

Many more of us are now finding ourselves being asked not only to attend more meetings; we are sometimes expected to manage them. This requirement is likely to increase as management structures flatten out and greater opportunities arise for us to become involved in creating and managing the discussions and decision-making processes that affect so many areas of our lives.

One of the difficulties is that relatively few people have excellent experiences of meetings or have good meeting skills to bring to bear when called upon to manage meetings. Surprisingly little training in meeting management seems to be offered in any field. There appears to be an expectation that when a person is good at their job and is promoted to manager, team leader or some role which requires them to manage meetings that the skills to do so effectively and effortlessly will suddenly emerge.

For business meetings to be efficient and for inspirational and essential projects in the Voluntary and Community Sector to be sustainable, the meetings through which they are organized need to be skillfully managed.

There is a growing need for competent, skilled people to manage these meetings. These skills can be easily learned and implemented and the role can become rewarding and fulfilling, especially when the outcomes improve situations or enhance lives.

If you are new to meeting management the information in this book could help you to become competent and confident. If you're already experienced in managing meetings the information might assist you in the further development of your skills.

Effectiveness and enjoyment in your meetings will be guaranteed simply by implementing the procedures and processes, the tools and techniques, embodying the skills and benefitting from the insights and experience offered in this book

Meeting Management

The purpose of any meeting is to bring two or more people together to achieve defined outcomes. These outcomes may be wide ranging, such as developing ideas for community regeneration, or be very specific e.g. allocating budgets to projects.

A fully effective meeting will achieve its purpose to the satisfaction of its participants in a smooth and efficient manner. It will complete the agenda, make sensible decisions and have beneficial outcomes. An enjoyable meeting will be interesting; everyone attending will feel included and valuable and have an equal opportunity to be heard and to contribute.

Whatever the form the meeting takes there will be a requirement for some elements of planning and management. The quality of the management of any meeting will have a huge influence on the outcomes. Poorly managed meetings can result in the failure of a project, the ineffectiveness of a group or organization and the frustration and dissatisfaction of the participants. Well managed meetings usually result in outcomes leading to the success of projects, the ongoing effectiveness of groups and organizations and leave participants feeling satisfied that they have spent their time wisely and productively.

Whether a meeting is for a few colleagues to briefly check in with one another on the progress of their work or a large gathering of people considering the future of their town, the basic principles of meeting management are more or less the same.

A Quick Guide to Meeting Management

Effective meeting management is finding the balance in fulfilling the purpose of the meeting within the agreed time, and encouraging appropriate contributions from all the participants, while making the meeting enjoyable and rewarding for all concerned.

Beforehand

While planning the meeting consider what would be the most suitable date, time and venue and which attendees ought to be to present to ensure successful outcomes. Be well prepared. Having everything in place and leaving as little as possible to chance can avoid stress and can lay the foundations for an enjoyable and productive meeting.

Starting the meeting

1. Start on time and state when the meeting will finish.
2. Thank everyone for attending and make introductions if appropriate.
3. Facilitate a process to help participants connect with one another.
4. Provide some context by briefly outlining the topics for discussion and clarify the main aims of the meeting and broad intended outcomes.
5. Gain agreements on such things as behavior, communication and confidentiality when appropriate.
6. Create the agenda or check that everyone has received the agenda and all other necessary information already sent out.

During the meeting

➢ Make the meeting a satisfactory experience for all involved.
➢ Promote an atmosphere of inclusion and make everyone feel involved and respected.
➢ Listen carefully to all contributions.
➢ Encourage participation.
➢ Facilitate balanced discussion.
➢ Encourage the reticent, support the reasonable, and suppress the overbearing.
➢ Stick to the agreed agenda/points for discussion.
➢ Keep people focused and the meeting on track and on time.
➢ Time manage questions and responses.
➢ Summarize succinctly, so that people are clear about what they are

deciding upon.

➤ Make any voting processes clear and efficient.

Closing the meeting

1. Sum up the meeting, stating the conclusions reached, the decisions made and any outcomes arising from the meeting.
2. Make clear what happens next and who is responsible for which steps.
3. Clarify arrangements for the next meeting.
4. Facilitate a brief process for participants to give feedback about the meeting.
5. Thank everyone for his or her attendance and show extra appreciation where appropriate.
6. Bring the meeting to a clear ending.
7. Finish on time.

Asking for feedback in meetings is frequently overlooked or left out. Receiving direct feedback from participants on how they experienced the meeting provides an opportunity for meeting managers to learn from the experience. Hearing about what worked or what did not; what was confusing, frustrating or enjoyable can help meeting managers to develop their skills.

Recording a meeting

It is often customary for a scribe or a secretary to produce minutes or a brief report of the meeting to send out to members of the group who were unable to attend and to other interested parties. In some circumstances minutes may need to be verified by the people present as being an accurate account of the meeting.

In some informal meetings this could be dispensed with. If they wish, participants could make their own notes of the proceedings to aid their memories.

After the meeting

Debriefing after a meeting is as important as preparation is beforehand.

Debriefing.

This debriefing could be done with a participant or with someone else whose judgment you trust. This is to support you in gaining some clear perspective of the meeting and its outcome.

Feedback received from participants will be valuable information to bring into the debriefing.

If debriefing with another person is not possible you can review the meeting by yourself. This is better than nothing.

Appreciation

Appreciating yourself is as important as recognizing the parts you might have done better or differently and far more productive than berating yourself for any perceived mistakes. Appreciate yourself for the work you have done. For the qualities you brought to the meeting. For the parts you did well. For your willingness to manage the meeting and for how much you learned from the experience.

> To be fully effective, meetings ought to be not only productive they ought also to be enjoyable for all those engaged in them; including the meeting manager!

The difference between chairing and facilitating

Whilst there may be some common factors in these roles they are two very distinctive methods and each is appropriate for particular circumstances. However, it could be useful to be open to the beneficial possibilities of bringing elements of each into the other.

The similarities

The similarities of these two roles are:
1. Focusing a group's attention upon the issues under discussion.
2. Productively exploring those issues as fully as possible within the meeting timeframe.
3. Eliciting contributions from attendees.
4. Supporting people to come to conclusion and agreed actions regarding those issues.
5. Creating agreement about the steps to be taken to implement the decisions reached.

The differences

These differences are mostly in the way the participants and the procedures are managed. Chaired meetings usually follow formal meeting protocols whilst facilitated meetings are less formal and more interactive.

The emphasis in chaired meeting tends to be upon results, whilst in facilitated meetings a great deal more attention is paid to the process.

While meeting managers in both roles ought to be evenhanded in giving time to various opinions on the issues under consideration, the chairperson is often more directive while the facilitator usually devises ways through which to encourage engagement. One main difference is that a chairperson customarily has a vote while a facilitator usually does not.

Chairing

Chaired meetings usually follow a formal structure which is customarily along the lines of or similar to parliamentary meeting procedures. The chairperson is clearly in charge and they are usually either elected or appointed to that position. Other officers - secretary and treasurer - will often be elected or appointed to serve with them. Apart from a few exceptions, such as Annual General Meetings, chaired meetings are typically small affairs, which are usually conducted around one table.

The dynamics of any chaired group are likely to have many similarities. Whether it is the board of a multinational conglomerate or the church fete committee, there are likely to be politics and ego at play. The chairperson may need to keep a firm grip on proceedings. It is their job to keep order, to focus attention and get the meeting to arrive at decisions. Some of the suggestions in the chapter on handling tricky situations could help to keep people on track.

The ability of a chairperson to slice through waffle and bring a group of people, often with opposing views, to an agreed conclusion can be extremely valuable, especially when time is a precious commodity or when people's physical or financial wellbeing are at stake.

I asked a well-known chairman of a national corporation what was the secret of being a successful chairman. He replied that it was the ability to make decisions.

In the decision-making process of most chaired meetings, the chairperson has a vote and their vote can often carry the decision. In some situations, the decisive use of their crucial vote may be what identifies an effective chairperson. However, there may arise a conflict of interest if the chairperson is deeply involved in the organization or is attached to a specific outcome of a meeting. In these circumstances a chairperson needs to be aware of the responsibilities of their role and avoid managing the proceedings in a manner that could influence the outcomes to suit their own personal agenda.

> Potential conflict of interest can lead to tensions in a group whose meetings are chaired by a group member. Some meetings could benefit from being chaired by an independent chairperson.

Characteristics of an effective chairperson

He or she:

➤ Embodies the ethics and values of the group or organization.
➤ Listens and communicates well.
➤ Encourages participation.
➤ Is impartial and flexible.
➤ Summarizes accurately and succinctly.
➤ Is diplomatic.
➤ Exercises authority and positive leadership when necessary.
➤ Avoids undue conflict.
➤ Gains consensus where possible.
➤ Achieves the aims of the meeting.
➤ Tenaciously ensures follow-through on actions.

The chairperson's role can be made more or less effective by the way in which the secretary to the meeting performs his or her role.

Characteristics of an effective secretary

He or she:

➤ Embodies the ethics and values of the group.
➤ Listens well.
➤ Is methodical and reliable.
➤ Is vigilant and has the ability for sustained concentration.
➤ Employs good writing skills.

Chairperson and secretary working together as a team:

➤ Agree a list of agenda items for the forthcoming meeting.
➤ Agree on logistics such as who will act as timekeeper.
➤ Debrief after meetings and agree who will check on any follow up item.
➤ Agree the minutes, notes or action points.

Before the meeting the chairperson or secretary is to:

a. Book the room and arrange for any equipment and refreshments.
b. Set the deadline for submissions for the agenda.
c. Identify matters arising from previous minutes.
d. Send out the agenda in good time for people to make any necessary preparations.
e. Indicate what the group/committee is required to do with that

information, for example to note, to gather information, to approve, to consider, to decide upon.

f. Prepare a list of apologies.

g. Arrive early to check the room and greet attendees and any presenters and observers.

Starting the meeting the chairperson is to:

1. Start on time and state when the meeting will finish.
2. Thank everyone for attending.
3. Make introductions and check that everyone has received the agenda and all other necessary papers.
4. Provide some context by briefly outlining the topics for discussion and clarify the main aims of the meeting and broad intended outcomes.
5. Read out any apologies.
6. Get the minutes of the last meeting adopted for the record.

During the meeting the chairperson is to:

- ➤ Make the meeting as enjoyable an experience as possible.
- ➤ Promote an atmosphere of inclusion and make everyone feel involved and respected.
- ➤ Enable participation by all members and presenters.
- ➤ Stick to the agreed agenda/points for discussion.
- ➤ Keep people focused and the meeting on track and on time. Have a clock visible to avoid the need to refer to a watch.
- ➤ Time manage questions.
- ➤ Time manage responses to questions.
- ➤ Give those questioned an opportunity to restate points or make additional comments.
- ➤ Listen carefully to all contributions.
- ➤ Facilitate balanced discussion.
- ➤ Sum up succinctly, so that people are clear about what they are hearing or deciding upon.
- ➤ Make voting processes clear and efficient.
- ➤ Discourage major items from coming up in 'any other business'.

The secretary is to:

- ➤ Be ready to invite visiting presenters to join the meeting.
- ➤ Be prepared, through the chair, to ask questions and require verification of any unclear point.
- ➤ Avoid distractions such as shuffling papers.
- ➤ If necessary ask for summing up of proposals to be voted upon.

> ➤ Ask for copies of any prepared presentations for inclusion with the minutes.

Closing the meeting the chairperson is to:

1. Sum up the meeting, stating the conclusions reached, the decisions made and any outcomes arising from the meeting.
2. Make clear what happens next and who is responsible for which steps.
3. Clarify arrangements for the next meeting.
4. Request feedback from participants on their experience of the meeting.
5. Thank everyone for his or her attendance and show appreciation where appropriate.
6. Bring the meeting to a clear ending.
7. Finish on time.
8. Do not be quick to leave.
9. Chairperson or the secretary makes sure the room is left in good order.
10. Chairperson and the Secretary arrange a debriefing.

> Feedback from participants is rarely requested during formal meetings. This might be why some chairperson's do not know that they are considered to be ineffective by participants. It may take courage to break with tradition and ask for feedback, however, the results could be well worth it.

After the meeting the secretary is to:

a. Meet with the chairperson to debrief the meeting.
b. Write up minutes as soon as possible and get the chairperson to check them. Take care to mention the people in attendance, those who sent apologies and those who were just absent. Actions arising need to be marked clearly with who will do what and by when.
c. Circulate these within five working days for people to check and return by a specific date.
d. Make any amendments to minutes as suggested by the meeting members. This way the approval of minutes at the next meeting becomes a mere formality.

Facilitating

The dictionary description of the word facilitate is: to make easy, to ease, to make possible, to smooth the progress, to help, to aid, to assist.

Facilitators do all of these in their meetings to achieve the most appropriate outcome for the participants. They make sure that all voices are heard, that people feel encouraged to make a contribution and are supported to think creatively. They select and manage processes for group exploration, discussion and decision-making.

Facilitated meetings can be simple affairs in which small groups of people discuss topics and issues of common interest or concern. They can also be large events through which awareness can be raised or where wide ranging opinions and experience can be sought. Facilitation is effective in handling very large events such as community meetings and public consultations.

> The role of the facilitator is to do just that; to facilitate the proceedings. They are to ensure that the topic of the meeting is explored as fully as possible and all participants have the opportunity to raise issues, voice concerns, offer ideas and solutions, and to feel a sense of ownership of decisions made.

While politics and ego are likely to also be present in these types of meetings, the processes used by the facilitator - as described in the chapter on Procedures and Processes - are designed to minimize the detrimental effect of these.

The role of the facilitator is to select and prepare the venue in the appropriate way to suit the occasion and the inclusion and accessibility of all the participants. The proceedings are usually conducted in a seated circle or in small circles of participants dotted around the room. Facilitated meetings can have some physical movement in them as participants are encouraged to explore the topic in a variety of ways with as many people as is possible or necessary.

Unlike the chairperson, who may have power to influence the outcome of their meetings, the attitude of the facilitator ought to be neutral and non-attached to any particular outcome. It is their role to ensure that the participants achieve the most appropriate results for themselves and by themselves.

In larger meetings or events it might be advisable for the facilitation to be handled by several people. Between them these co-facilitators manage the various roles of leading processes, timekeeping, observing attitudes, behavior and the mood in the room and recording progress.

One person can handle the facilitation of small meetings, although, it can be more effective to have co-facilitators or people in the support roles of scribe and timekeeper. In regular group meetings members could take each of these roles on in rotation. This gives everyone the opportunity to practice these roles and prevents them from becoming onerous tasks.

The formula for an effectively facilitated meeting

Whether a meeting is being run as a large group event or a small group discussion, a well-facilitated meeting will follow a similar formula:

1. A clear beginning.
2. A clarification of the purpose and the intended outcomes.
3. Appropriate introductions.
4. Suitable processes, some of which will follow on from and build upon the one previous.
5. Full participation of all participants.
6. A summing up of what has been achieved at the meeting.
7. Clarification of the next steps to be taken by whom and by when.
8. Appreciations in general and in specifics.
9. A clear ending.

The facilitator's role is to:
➢ Serve the participants.
➢ Be evenhanded and impartial with all attendees.
➢ Select and manage the processes.
➢ Use the essential tools of clear communication, firm timekeeping, a respectful attitude and non-attachment to the outcomes.

Planning the meeting

Planning the meeting will include: the date and time, the venue, the logistics, the timings and the strategies of the meeting. Where appropriate, attention will be needed to identify members of stakeholder groups to be approached.

Inclusive meetings

In order to make the greatest possible difference, meetings ought to be as inclusive as possible. An inclusive meeting is one that is designed to be open and accessible to a wide diversity of people and which provides equal opportunities for contributions from all participants.

How inclusive is inclusive?

Inclusion is, of course, relative. All meetings, because of their content, venue or timing are relatively open or closed. The most closed are when small groups of people, such as single race, single sex, specialist, professional or like-minded individuals make decisions that affect the lives of people who have no voice in the meeting.

Inclusive meetings are assemblies in which different kinds of people gather together to discover how they can cooperate to make decisions or bring about mutually advantageous decisions.

Some limits to inclusion come from physical conditions and timing factors. For example, holding meetings in places inaccessible to wheelchairs will obviously exclude wheelchair users; meetings that take place during working hours could exclude many full time workers. Saturdays will usually be difficult for retailers and those regularly participating or working in leisure activities.

The timing of a meeting can be crucial to its success. Awareness of some of the key dates that may affect potential participants is essential. Seasonal pressures can preclude some people from attending events at certain times of the year i.e. school holidays might exclude many parents.

Although attending meetings that happen only in the evenings may prove difficult for some parents and carers, this is often the best option for including the greatest number of people in a meeting to address community concerns.

Meetings are most effective when comparatively relaxed and free from pressure and where there is capacity to pay attention to the special needs of the participants. The format of these meetings will include processes that support inclusion, for example an initial Go-Round in which participants can describe their special needs. This may lead to such things as more supportive chairs being found for those with bad backs, a sighted person helping a sight-impaired person, presenters taking more care to speak clearly for the people for whom English is not their first language, people who need to leave early having their exit respectfully facilitated and so on.

These methods and processes support a structure for meetings that can make the most of having a diverse mix of participants. These meetings can then benefit from wide perspectives, a broader ownership, cross-cultural synergies and access to otherwise excluded sections of an organization or community.

Participation in inclusive meetings

Who the participants in a meeting are and how they behave will influence which processes will be chosen for ensuring free-flowing discussion, keeping order, efficient decision-making and the eventual outcome of the meeting.

Most meetings will benefit from having as comprehensive a variety of skills, information and experience as possible amongst its participants.

On the face of it, it may seem advantageous for all the people at a meeting to share the same opinions and to agree with the ways in which goals could be achieved. In my experience, while that may result in quick, comfortable and easy meetings, it may not achieve the best results for the greatest number of people in the long run.

Opposing views might create conflict or bring some disharmony to a meeting; they also may bring a richness of options. Through the highlighting of concerns and the quizzing about ideas and the requesting of the details in suggestions, issues can be more thoroughly explored and a refinement brought to decision-making.

Leaving out people who might be difficult to handle or who are likely to have differing views to the majority, may result in short-term gain over long-term pain. Those people, who are unintentionally excluded from meetings where decisions will be taken that will affect them, may feel disappointed, disempowered, angry or resentful. People who believe they have been deliberately excluded might feel motivated to oppose the implementation of any decisions taken in their absence. They may put a lot of time and effort into undermining or sabotaging any outcome of such a meeting.

Remember the fairy story about sleeping beauty? It was the fairy that was not invited to the celebration that cast the spell that caused so much trouble in the kingdom!

Good, inclusive meetings can achieve high productivity and provide people with a conscious sense of ownership from participating in such events.

Care ought to be taken to employ methods and processes that ensure all participants can make their contribution with ease.

In my experience, the smallest methods and simplest processes can be easily applied to any meeting, especially within established groups or organizations. This simple approach can radically change attitudes and set in motion the transformation towards inclusivity of a group or organization's meeting culture.

Notification

When the planning is completed the venue is booked and any equipment and materials acquired. Notification of the meeting ought to go out in a number of ways and in plenty of time for people to organize their attendance.

Setting up and starting the meeting

Arrive in plenty of time to set the room up and prepare any necessary equipment and materials. Facilitated meetings are usually held within a circle or in the case of larger meetings in a number of smaller circles. (These could be made of random groups or specific interest or stakeholder groups). This is to allow people to easily see the people with whom they are working. Anything that participants need to make the event enjoyable, comfortable and productive ought to be made easily available.

When to postpone, cancel or carry on

If few participants show up you will have to decide whether to postpone, cancel or carry on with a meeting. The decision may be a difficult one to make because of some factors and implications. Use common sense, use your intuition and discuss the decision with those involved.

Many years ago I convened a local community meeting in a town in Northern Scotland to which many stakeholder representatives had been invited, as had a team of outside facilitator's. This was the first meeting in the planning of a Future Search event to consider an important community wide issue.

A blizzard had been blowing throughout the day making the roads almost impassable and cancelling public transport. The independent facilitators, who had driven for most of the day through these appalling conditions, only arrived a short while before the meeting was due to start.

By this time there were only a handful of participants in the hall. We wondered if this was it? Would anyone else arrive? Were no more people interested in the topic or had they been delayed or understandably put off by the weather? This being a rural community some people would have to travel miles to the event. Ought we to postpone the meeting, cancel it altogether or just have a discussion amongst the people who were there?

We decided to continue with the meeting. Within a short while another 100 or so people arrived. Some of them had trudged for miles through the snow. Others had come on skis, sledges and tractors. People with chains on their tires had made several journeys to ferry people to the meeting.

This event turned out to be one of the most significant and productive meetings to be held in the area. The interest that was stimulated in the topic continued for years with many beneficial outcomes for the whole community.

Start on time

> Start on time to honor the commitment and efficient time-keeping of all those who are present.

Greet latecomers with a smile and have them be integrated into the meeting with as little fuss and interruption to the proceedings as possible.

The first part of the meeting is all about setting the scene and making people feel comfortable with what lies ahead. Some sort of ice-breaking activity, such as a co-operative game, can release tension and help people to connect with one another.

Being open and clear about the procedure and processes, what you intend to do and why will help people to focus on the content of the meeting rather than the facilitation. The most important part of starting any meeting is to ensure that participants gain a clear understanding of the meeting purpose and aims.

Introductions
The facilitator/s:
1. Introduces themselves and explains their role.
2. Welcomes the participants and appreciates them for investing their time in the meeting.
3. Provides a brief outline of why the meeting is being held and any necessary background information.
4. Provides a brief outline of what kind of results or outcomes the meeting is intended to achieve.
5. Indicates how long the meeting will take.
6. Talks briefly about how they intend to run the proceedings, for example brainstorming, goal setting, discussion groups etc.
7. Emphasizes that their role is to manage the process and to ask questions.
8. Emphasize that they will be drawing on the skills and experience of those present to develop agreed solutions.

The participants:
Are asked to introduce themselves to one another:
- Their names.
- Who they represent, if appropriate.
- Where they are from, if appropriate.
- Why they are at the meeting.
- What they hope to get out of it.

The meeting procedures
1. Ground rules or group agreements are made.
2. An open agenda is created. (See Creating Agendas in the chapter on Procedures and Processes).
3. A variety of processes are used to engage participants in the topics and help them to achieve their goals.
4. Options for decisions are summarized.
5. These are thoroughly and openly explored.
6. Votes are taken, if appropriate.
7. Next steps are identified.
8. What will be done by whom and by when is agreed-upon.

Ending the meeting

The facilitator concludes the meeting by:

1. Summing up the proceedings.
2. Identifying the next steps to be taken by when and by whom.
3. Receiving feedback from the participants about their experience of the meeting.
4. Appreciating the participants for their participation and any co-facilitator's and guest presenters for their support and contribution.
5. Announcing the venue and the date of the next meeting, if appropriate.
6. Bringing the meeting to clear ending.
7. Finishing on time.
8. Arranging a debrief meeting with their co-facilitator/s or a support person.
9. Leaving the room in good order.

Virtual Meetings

Technology has had an impact on meetings - it has allowed for the creation of Virtual Meetings. As people do not need to travel to these meetings, which saves time and energy, an increasing number of meetings are now being held virtually. This allows people to have group discussions, even when they are miles or even continents apart. They can 'meet' via a variety of technologies.

However, in many cases, the unfortunate attitudes, poor-levels of communication skills and inappropriate behavior that have traditionally resulted in dysfunctional and ineffective meetings are sometimes still there. In fact these are often made considerably worse by the time delays of satellite connections and the lack of feelings of real connection between people.

Any person who has difficulties managing conventional meetings is unlikely to fair much better in virtual ones.

As well as the fundamentals already described there are few extra things regarding timing and clarity of communication to bear in mind in virtual meetings.

 Things to remember:
  ➤ Be mindful of the variation in time zones around the world and the effect that could have on people's concentration.
  ➤ Keep a conscious awareness of the unavoidable pauses produced by the length of time for some signal transmissions. Allow for this when managing discussions and when calculating the length of time for the meeting.

> ➤ To prevent the chaos of several people speaking at the same time, have clearly understood procedures for making contributions. This could be as simple as the traditional meeting method of only speaking when invited to by the meeting manager.
> ➤ Whenever possible have a clear running order of speakers or presentations and stick to it.

There seems to be a tendency in virtual meetings for people to join and leave with a casualness that would not be appropriate or acceptable in traditional meetings. Some people have been known to make their points and opinions known and then break connection before hearing those of others. This can have the unfortunate effect of devaluing meetings and the outcomes from them. To avoid this, be very clear about the start and finish times of the meeting and ask for a commitment from all participants to be available during those times. Create a clear agenda and send it out well before the meeting and stick to it. If on some rare occasion a participant will need to leave the virtual meeting early, they could make their needs known ahead of time so that this could be factored into the agenda and running order. Transcriptions or other forms of recording virtual meetings could be circulated afterwards.

Making the difference as a facilitator

There are several ways in which you can make a significant difference to the proceedings:

Be Yourself

Be real. Show up as yourself. Avoid taking on the persona of the 'expert'. Use your strengths and acknowledge your weaknesses. Give any activity in which you are not skilled over to others who are.

Be present

Be fully and completely present for the group. It shows, and participants will notice. Listen attentively, while observing with your peripheral vision. Be aware of who is in the room and what is happening. Use all of the available space.

Selecting the processes

Processes, games and activities are means to an end – not the end in itself. What is important is to know what end you are aiming for or what behavioral change or shift you are facilitating. Then the selection of activities becomes easy. Every activity is an opportunity to learn, to share and to grow.

Spontaneity

By all means research your group, know their objectives, prepare yourself, the space and materials you may need. However, do not be too attached to your plan. Try facilitating without a plan. Be spontaneous. Try it and see what happens. You may surprise yourself and delight the group with your spontaneity!

Do something

When in doubt about what to do next, just do something. Stop thinking. Stop analyzing. Do not try and be clever or funny. Just do something and start anywhere with the first thing that comes to mind – then build on it. Use your body. Move around or ask the group to do so. Get a different perspective. Trust yourself and the participants.

Take risks

Growth comes from what is learned through taking risks. Whether or not they work, take a bow. And then do something else. Take more risks – try something new.

Make mistakes

Acknowledge 'failure' – to yourself and others. Realizations that arise from these are to be celebrated. Acknowledge that something didn't work and move on. This is one way of remaining present. If you are dwelling on something that didn't work in the last process, you will not be fully present in the next one.

It is not about you

It is important to remember that your role is to help people to reach their objectives, not to show how clever you are or how many activities you know. It's not about you – it's about the participants. Many people are starved for the types of interactions that facilitated meetings provide. They get to express themselves creatively, play together, examine their thoughts, have their voices heard, have their extreme ideas and their failures forgiven or celebrated.

Let go

Let go of the need to control. That is based on fear. Trust yourself. Trust the wisdom of the group. Trust your knowledge of and skills with processes. Provide a structure of support for the group's endeavors and then let them get on with the work they have to do. Be comfortable with uncertainty and believe that what emerges is what is supposed to emerge.

When it's over let it be over. After debriefing and noting what you have learned, let go and move on.

 Things to remember

About the participants:
- ➢ People are the most complex creatures on the planet.
- ➢ Each participant is likely to have his or her personal agenda, which may be hidden; sometimes even from them!
- ➢ No matter how tempting you make the water seem, the horses you lead to it must **want** to drink it.
- ➢ People have a right to feel what they feel regardless of what sense that makes to anybody else.
- ➢ People have a right to their opinions and beliefs, no matter how irrational they may seem.
- ➢ People can only change their own minds.
- ➢ Never underestimate the power of a small group to bring about change.

About yourself:
- ➢ You can only do your best.
- ➢ This is all that can be expected by you or by anybody else.
- ➢ Fear and nervousness are excitement waiting to get out.
- ➢ Sometimes all you need to do is breathe. Breathe in; breathe out – it's easy!
- ➢ Mistakes are only learning opportunities.
- ➢ You will grow and improve with every meeting.

Be the difference

The Facilitation of events could be your chosen way to make a difference and bring about positive change. If so, the most effective way of achieving that is to model the difference you wish to encourage. Through learning, developing, integrating and demonstrating constructive communication, cooperative and inclusive working practices, compassion, high moral values and ethics you can be an inspiration to others.

Whenever possible within your events remember to also have fun!

When you do, those around you are likely to have fun too and your meetings and events will be the ones people enjoy and ones in which they will be eager to participate in the future.

Becoming more proficient

As increasing numbers of people expect to be facilitated in meetings, rather than be chaired, there is a growing need for skilled facilitators. For this reason I have written: EFFORTLESS FACILITATION, in the YOU MAKE THE DIFFERENCE series. This is available in paperback and e-book format from Amazon and accessible through our website: www.youmakethedifference.net

If you wish to deepen your knowledge of the methods and procedures involved in designing and facilitating excellent meetings and events or to further improve your skills as a facilitator you might find this volume interesting and useful.

2

PROCEDURES AND PROCESSES

All of the following procedures and processes can be used in the facilitation of meetings and events. Many of them can also be used to good effect in chaired meetings, perhaps more than you would imagine.

Realizing that many participants now expect meetings to be interactive, wise chairpersons in the voluntary and community sector are relaxing the rigid formality of their meetings wherever possible and incorporating processes for creating inclusivity.

As corporate structures flatten out more people in business organizations are using a variety of processes within meetings to engage staff in decision-making and the development of trust and teamwork.

Procedures for beginning meetings

Clear beginnings make it obvious to participants that the proceedings have started which now require the full focus of their attention.

Creative use of flip-charts or whiteboards can be beneficial
– have fun!

An Opening Moment of Silence

At the beginning of a meeting or an event it can be useful to start by taking a Moment of Silence. This can give everyone time to fully arrive and gather thoughts in preparation for what lies ahead.

Instructions

These can be as simple, or as elaborate as you feel the participants need. An opening moment of silence could be facilitated along these lines: 'before we begin, let's just take a moment to catch our breath/bring ourselves fully here/gather our thoughts/etc. Please put your belongings down on the floor; sit up straight in your chairs with both feet on the floor.' (Pause) 'It might be helpful for you to lower or close your eyes and feel yourself

23

beginning to relax. Take a few deep breaths and release from your mind all that has been involved in getting here. Concentrate on taking slow deep breathes. As you slowly breathe out you can let go of any anxiety and stress and then breathe in a sense of peace and calmness.'

After a short while (thirty seconds to a couple of minutes depending on how experienced the participants are in this kind of activity) suggest, 'now begin to once more become aware of this room and those around you.'

Then, after a few more seconds say, 'Thank you. Please open your eyes and look around the room making eye contact with some of the people with whom you will be spending the next hour/few hours/day, etc...' The meeting then proceeds.

Benefits

Taking this moment gives people the opportunity to catch their breath after the journey or after rushing from a previous meeting, to relax and to feel comfortable with their surroundings.

Challenges

Some people are uncomfortable with silence. Others might mistakenly believe that an effective meeting is one that starts with business and rushes through to complete the agenda. These people may think that any pauses in the proceedings are a waste of time.

Some people might consider the use of a moment of silence to be 'flaky' and somehow not businesslike or professional. These people may need reassuring that these moments of pause, of silence, are intelligent uses of time and are often the most effective way of assisting participants to be fully present and engaged in the proceedings to come.

The taking of a moment of silence at the beginning of a meeting blew my mind with its effectiveness when I first came across it in the late 1980s. Although, since then it has become a valued process in many types of meetings, it is still relatively rare in business and traditionally run meetings.

> The benefits of an opening moment of silence to the participants and to the proceedings are so many that they outweigh any reasons for reticence.

Welcoming procedures and processes

Meeting purpose

> The reason for and the purpose of the meeting ought to be clearly stated, as are any hoped for or intended outcomes.

Housekeeping

Be sure that the following aspects are covered and it can be useful to display these creatively on a flip chart:

HOUSEKEEPING

ORIENTATION, COMFORT BREAKS

RULES OF THE HOUSE

RESPECT THE POLICY, EXCEPTIONS

REFRESHMENT BREAKS

APPROXIMATE TIMING OF THE DAY

LUNCH BREAK

FIRE ALARM INSTRUCTIONS

ANY ANNOUNCEMENTS

Overview of the meeting

Briefly go through what is to be covered in the meeting. Mention any proposed breaks. Indicate the intended finishing time. If you think it might be necessary ask if there could be a little flexibility around that and if there is anyone who needs to leave earlier than that time.

Making agreements

Ask for agreements from participants on timekeeping, on confidentiality around personal matters and anything else that seems appropriate.

Introduction processes

There are a number of ways in which participants in a meeting can introduce themselves to one another. The method chosen will depend on a number of factors such as whether this is a regular meeting, how formal it needs to be, how well people already know one another or if there are one or more strangers or visitors present. It is usual for the meeting manager to introduce themselves first, then any co-managers and guests. Then the participants can introduce themselves.

Go-Rounds

Most meetings can start with a Go-Round of introductions which allows everyone at the meeting to introduce themselves in turn starting with the meeting manager and then the person to their left or right. The Go-Round is completed when everyone in the circle has spoken.

At the beginning of a meeting or where people are coming together for the first time a Go-Round needs to be simple, 'say your name and one thing about yourself' or 'your name and where you live' are examples.

> When appropriate, include a question about why people have come and what they hope to achieve from the meeting; especially if you are unsure what the participants expect.

For facilitators, these Go-Rounds can provide the information that is required to improvise or devise any fine-tuning to the meeting design. Better a slightly altered meeting than an irrelevant one!

Applications

A Go-Round is a multipurpose process that can have many other applications than introductions. These include putting forward ideas and suggestions, making brief presentations, expressing opinions, contributing to managed discussions, review, evaluation and feedback.

Paired introductions

This is a useful process, which has the added benefits of breaking the ice, getting people immersed in animated conversation and helping newcomers or strangers to get to know one other participant in some detail.

Step one

In the opening circle, participants pair up with someone. Either the person sitting next to them or preferably someone they do not know well. If the numbers of participants are uneven, the meeting manager partners up with a participant.

Each pair then takes turns in introducing themselves to each other with such things as:

1. Their name.
2. Where they are from.
3. The reason they came to the meeting.

4. Some topic they would like to have addressed.
5. The result they would like to see achieved by the end of the meeting.
6. Something they might want to say about themselves.

Allow around 2 minutes per person for this.

Step two

In a Go-Round in the circle each person introduces their partner to the group by repeating what they heard them say about themselves. One to two minutes per person ought to be long enough for this. People will probably describe the other person and their skills and experience with more enthusiasm than that person might do for himself or herself. This can be useful for mapping the skills available to the meeting.

Name games

In a meeting of a large number of participants the provision of nametags is useful. In other situations there may be occasions when name games could prove more beneficial, such as when people are to work together over a series of meetings, when the ice needs to be broken to create relaxation and harmony, when there are more than 12 and less than 24 participants, (less than 12 names can usually be remembered and more than 24 will need name tags).

To strengthen the memory of everyone's name, people can participate in one of the many simple games that offer opportunities for names to be repeated until they are remembered. One example is where participants stand up and throw a ball around the circle saying their own name as they throw the ball to someone. After a while this can be changed so that the person throwing the ball says the name of the person to whom they throw it. Not only does this activity help with name recognition, it raises energy levels and breaks the ice.

A variety of games for other situations are described later in this section.

Procedures for creating agendas

Traditional Agendas

In most traditional meetings access to constructing the agenda is often restricted to a few people. In formal meetings the agenda is usually created by the chairperson or the secretary and sent out to potential attendees some time before the meeting.

This method may be appropriate for meetings that are required to follow strict protocols. These types of meetings are usually ones where the people present are legally or financially accountable to other people. These are usually committee meetings, annual general meetings or meetings in which constitutional items will be discussed. The Constitution or Articles of Association of a group or an organization may require officers to be elected and to manage the meetings. These kinds of meetings usually follow a structure based on democratic Parliamentary procedure, which require an agenda to be sent to attendees some time prior to the meeting.

In formal and semi-formal meetings the agenda that has been sent is read out at the start of the meeting. The first item on the agenda, after any apologies are mentioned, will be the reading of the minutes of the last meeting and the adoption of them for the record. Any matters referred to in those minutes will need to be dealt with unless they are somewhere else on the agenda. The rest of the agenda will usually be followed in the order it is written. Occasionally the order might need to be changed to accommodate some circumstance.

Visible agendas

Apart from the most formal and rigidly structured meetings most meetings could benefit from having the agenda easily visible to all participants at all times during the meeting. To achieve this, the meeting manager or recorder writes the agenda on a flip chart or whiteboard where everyone can see it. Sometimes a visible timetable is a useful, separate addition to the agenda.

This method keeps the agenda in full view and allows the participants to keep track of the progress of the meeting more easily than when the agenda is on individual sheets of paper for each participant.

Application

This method works for most meeting situations and especially in inclusive and interactive types of meetings

Challenges

This may be a challenge to those people who are used to attending the more traditional form of meeting that usually adheres to rigid protocols and procedures.

Externally set agendas can produce problems for meetings. If, for example, a management group in an organization sets the agenda for a meeting of subordinates, the agenda may miss the opportunity to stimulate the creative thinking of the subordinate group. The subordinates, who may be in closer touch with the conditions on the ground, may have to struggle past possibly irrelevant agenda items before they can get to what it is the meeting ought to address.

When meeting managers preset the agenda, the dangers of irrelevant items or of mistaken priorities might be present.

> Note: Participants may find it difficult to fully respect an agenda that they have not had a part in creating.

Open Agenda

This is a powerful method which allows for collective construction of meetings and the timing of agenda items.

Working with an Open Agenda is an efficient and inclusive way to ensure that meetings have real relevance for the participants and a greater potential for achieving the intended outcomes. With an Open Agenda the whole group can be aware of any need to rework timings, priorities, breaks, etc., if the need arises. In this way the participants have some responsibility for the progress of the meeting.

Constructing an Open Agenda

At the beginning of the meeting the facilitator solicits items for the agenda from participants and these are written up as a Mind Map on a flip chart or white board.

Mind Maps

Mind Maps are free hand diagrams that start from a circle in the middle of a page in which the title of the topic is written. Items, ideas and suggestions are grouped around this hub. Lines radiating out at angles link these bubbles of topics, items and ideas to the central hub, like spokes on a wheel.

A Mind Map gives a visual representation of topics and allows the main points to be easily identified. It is a flexible way of presenting information that allows for alteration much more easily than lists and linear text.

Challenges

Mind mapping is a skill that may benefit from a bit of practice, as the mapper might have to translate sentences into keywords.

Applications

Mind maps have many applications:

➢ Any occasion where notes are required.
➢ In preparation for presentations.
➢ In recording or preparing response to presentations.
➢ Planning meetings.
➢ Creating agendas.
➢ Planning a party, a holiday or any complex task.
➢ Reviewing thinking.

Creating a Mind Map as the agenda for a meeting is a relatively easy task. The purpose of the meeting is written in the centre of the map and a circle is drawn around it. As the items are called out by the participants they are written concisely somewhere on the map, circled and linked to the hub like the spokes of a wheel. Related items can be clustered together showing the links between them. Different colored markers could be used to easily distinguish each item.

The mind map method permits participants to brainstorm items for an agenda without any constraints about the order or timing or priorities. Nor does the position of an item on a mind map indicate its importance.

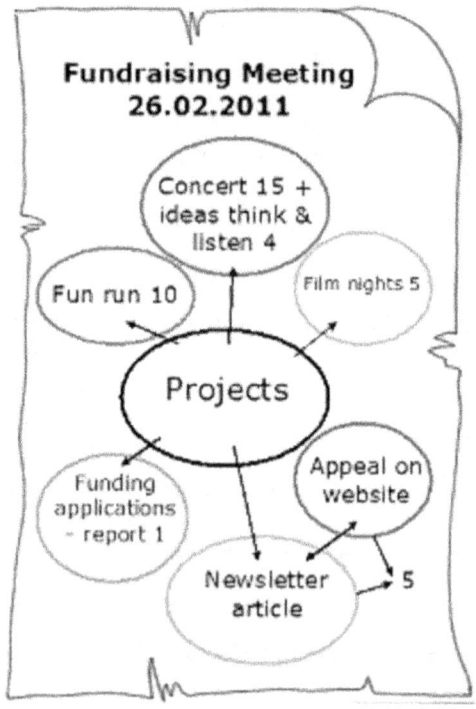

Timing
Check-In and introduction of any new members **5-10** minutes
Creating agenda **5** minutes
Dealing with items **40-50** minutes
Summing up and confirming next steps **5** minutes
Feedback **5** minutes
Total meeting time approximately **60-75** minutes.

Categorizing

The group is then facilitated to categorize whether each item on the map requires short, medium or long amounts of attention. Based on the time available for the meeting and the number of agenda items to be covered, a rough calculation can be made. Short items might be five minutes, medium 10 minutes and long 20 minutes. The relevant time allocations are written next to each item.

Some very brief items might show up at this stage and these need to be accommodated. For example there may be a short report that no action has been taken on an issue since the last meeting or that a piece of information is not yet available.

> Note: often items that are flagged up as 'this only needs a minute' turn out to take much longer than predicted.

Running order

The group is now ready to decide a running order. Referring to this stage as 'the running order' rather than prioritization, avoids the assumption that the longer items are of the greatest importance and must go first, which may not be the case. Generally, short items go first otherwise these may get left out if the longer items for discussion take more time than expected. Covering short and easy items first creates a sense of getting things done and generates an atmosphere of accomplishment. However, care must be taken to keep to the agreed timings to avoid losing time needed for the longer discussions.

Monitoring progress

During the meeting the facilitator, recorder or timekeeper will draw participants' attention to progress against the plan. Adjustments can be made. For example, an item that was allocated a medium amount of time and now appears to need longer, could gain some time from items that have taken less than their allotted time. Or the group may decide to move that item to the agenda of the next meeting where it can be given a more appropriate amount of time.

The participants agree any adjustments necessary in order to make the meeting a success.

Crossing out items as they are completed provides a sense of achievement, while reminding participants of what is still left to be handled.

Benefits

In my experience having all the participants of a meeting engaged in generating their Open Agenda on the spot and managing the priorities and timing of the items has many benefits over the traditional agenda method.

Frustration arising from dealing with irrelevant items is much more likely to derail a meeting and doggedly plodding through items without due consideration to appropriate timing can cause meetings to overrun. Mutual ownership of the agenda and meeting process gained through constructing Open Agendas can increase commitment to progressing the agenda to completion.

Working on constructing the agenda allows all participants to own the content. The method provides for any negotiations about the timing needed for items to be conducted in the open.

Understanding that the agenda timings and order can be reworked as necessary gives participants the security and confidence arising from a robust yet flexible structure.

Such an agenda is always relevant to participants needs and is strong evidence of the desire to devolve power and control.

An Open Agenda can be created for most meetings, even formal ones, as long as the necessary items required by the Constitution or Articles of Association appear. The use of these principles of flexibility and openness can work in all meetings even in the most tightly structured events. Doing so, even in very small doses, will change the character of an event from passive to active participation.

Challenges

Some people new to this process may think that it is a waste of time and that the time it takes could be used to process some items. These people may need reassurance that the process is likely to save time in the long run.

Participants may generate a wildly optimistic number of items for the agenda in the first place. However, as the stages of constructing the agenda unfold this will become obvious. It might be useful to engage in negotiations to pare down the number of items or do more of them as half-minute items.

> Items can be described briefly by their proposers in order to assist participants in deciding whether they ought to be included or not, although watch out for people 'doing' the agenda item in this phase of the meeting.

Alternatively, suggestions can be limited to one agenda item per person. Items requiring preparations of information or materials ought to have been flagged up in a previous meeting.

General processes

Check-In

From time to time a meeting manager will need to know how the participants at a meeting or an event are doing. How are people feeling after lunch or a long discussion? Are people warm/cool enough? Is there enough fresh air? Do people need a break? Can people keep going for another 10 minutes to finish this item before lunch?

The usual form for Check-In to take is a Go-Round. Going round the circle, each participant responds to whatever question the facilitator has asked. This of course will be required to be in an 'I' statement, such as 'I feel good after the lunch break' 'I'm feeling a bit tired now' 'I got a bit lost in the last discussion' 'I am glad that this was brought out into the open' 'I prefer that we continued for another 10 minutes to finish this item'.

Applications:

An occasional Check-In can help participants to continue to feel fully present in the meeting and lets them know that facilitators care about the state of their energy and comfort. A Check-In also provides facilitators with essential feedback to use in judging how to proceed.

Checking in with participants from time to time will help facilitators to gauge the mood of the meeting in order to provide the most appropriate processes and opportunities for reaching the group's goal.

Useful times for checking in are at the end of a period of deep concentration, when groups reconvene after separate activities, after lunch or when startling or distressing information has been disclosed.

Check-In methods
1 to 10

This is useful for a quick check-In. Participant say how they are feeling on a scale from 1 to 10 – 1 being the worst and 10 being the best.

Weather report

Another useful quick Check-In method is a 'weather report' Go-Round. Everyone states how he or she is feeling as though they are giving a report on themselves as the weather. 'Calm and clear', 'Sunny with a possibility of showers', 'Foggy', 'Stormy with lightening expected'. This can be an amusing, safer and surprisingly accurate way for people to be more honest about their feelings than by talking openly about them. It can be helpful in situations where there is unexpressed emotion lurking under the surface. A lot of 'rain' around can indicate distress and 'stormy weather' can point toward dissatisfaction or anger that will need to be addressed.

Thumbs up

When there is time only for a very quick Check-In, instead of everyone speaking in a Go-Round, the 'thumbs' method is a swift alternative. For example, for knowing the energy level of the group: 'show your thumbs up if you have good energy levels, thumbs down if you need a break and put your thumb somewhere in between to show how you are feeling'.

This is an improvement over just asking the question and getting a response from only one or two participants, which may be vague such as 'fine' or 'okay'.

Bringing attention to participant's energy and comfort will often stimulate them to do something about it - like opening a window. They might also be more willing to find extra energy for a short time, even when they are tired.

Temperature check

There is often a need to gauge the general mood in the room. Is it time to take a break, move on to the next item, stay with the new issue that has just come up, take a vote, extend the length of the meeting by an agreed amount of time in order to finish the discussion, etc. A show of hands may be all that is needed. However in large meetings it can be easier to count pieces of paper held aloft. If a 'temperature check' is likely to be a taken several times in a meeting then each participant could be issued with 2 sheets of colored paper, green for 'yes' and red for 'no' for example.

Challenges

Some people may not be used to describing how they feel or how they are getting on. This is cultural conditioning, which can soon break down as people feel heard and they notice how refreshing it is when they don't have to pretend that everything is always satisfactory for them.

Think and Listen

A Think and Listen session is a supportive process, which, with Go-Rounds, provides a good basis for inclusive, engaging and productive meetings. It can be used to help participants become clear in their minds what they think about something.

Think and Listen is a versatile method due to its simplicity, the small amount of time it takes and the many benefits arising from putting aside time to think.

There are many possible applications:

➤ To think up ideas or suggestions.

➤ To allow people to explore further what they already know about a situation, an issue or a topic.

➤ To generate comments or questions after a presentation.

➤ To stimulate options for decision-making.

➤ For considering and choosing between options.

➤ For making commitments to action.

This process allows people to try out new ideas, abandoning those with little promise, and settling on those with real potential, safe in the knowledge that the wanderings of their thoughts are private and confidential. Subsequently, when the meeting manager requests views, suggestions, questions or solutions regarding the topic in hand, the participant's will have already marshaled their thoughts, explored ideas and options and have their opinions ready to be expressed. Suggestions and feedback are likely to be more thorough and useful than they would have been without a Think and Listen session.

Think and Listen also gives people some opportunity to talk about what is going on. They may have been listening to presentation, carefully taking in what has been said. Now they can reverse the flow by speaking out their thoughts to another person. This can greatly improve their grasp of information and can alleviate fatigue that often comes from prolonged attentiveness.

Putting aside time to think

In conventional meetings people are usually expected to think on their feet. They are likely to have to make comments or take decisions before they have had a chance to think a matter through. Several results can flow from this: The person in the spotlight who has to do their thinking out loud, in public, might take a considerable chunk of airtime wandering around the topic searching for something useful to say. Other participants may grow impatient with this meandering and feel the need to shout down the speaker on the grounds that they are wasting time. Or they may override the speaker by putting forward their own views and so interrupt the speaker's train of thought. The speaker may never be able to come to a conclusion to their own satisfaction or finish what they want to say before the proceedings have to move on.

Another affect is to cause delivery of hurried decisions or poorly considered opinions as speakers attempt to avoid exposing any raw or preliminary thinking to the crowd by plumbing hastily for the first plausible view they can find.

Some people may not be able to cope with the spotlight of attention on them and so pass up the opportunity to participate merely to avoid exposure.

All of these diminish the quality of the group's efforts and work against participation and diversity of thinking. Preceding all decision-making and any opinion gathering with a process in which each participant has the opportunity to explore their own thoughts in safety can prevent these.

The process

During the Think and Listen session everyone at the meeting addresses a topic that has been proposed by the meeting manager, who also describes the process and ensures that everyone understands it.

Participants work in pairs. For half the allotted time one person is the thinker and the other person is the listener. At halftime the roles are reversed. The meeting manager handles the timing, which can be 2 to 5 minutes per person.

Thinking

The thinking turn is for the thinker's benefit. It provides them with an opportunity to think out loud in a supportive setting. It allows the thinker to collect and develop their thoughts about the topic at their own pace, in their own way. In mixed culture groups some people might feel more comfortable using their own language.

Help the thinkers to remember:
➤ This time is for them.
➤ It is for them to become clear in their thoughts regarding the topic.
➤ They do not need to appear bright or knowledgeable.
➤ They do not have to make sense to their partner.

Listening

The listener is there to offer a supportive space for their partner to think into. During this time the listener makes no comments and asks no questions. They do not need to understand the thinker and whether they agree or disagree with anything the thinker says is irrelevant. They can however, make encouraging sounds and movements such as nodding their head, to indicate that the thinker has their full attention.

Help the listeners to remember:
> ➤ To look at their partner while they listen.
> ➤ Be active in their listening through nodding their head or making encouraging noises.
> ➤ Not to interrupt or ask questions.
> ➤ Not to make comments or express opinion.
> ➤ If they disagree with what is said, they keep it to themselves.
> ➤ If they agree, they keep it to themselves.
> ➤ To keep their partner's thoughts confidential.

Confidentiality
What the thinker speaks about and how their thinking develops are kept confidential, known only to themselves and the listener. The listener makes no reference to what has been said by their thinking partner, either to the thinker or to anyone else, unless the thinker clearly gives permission. Within this ring of confidence there are no comments and no judgments.

When people relax into a Think and Listen session they find having an attentive, supportive and patient listener helps the quality of their thinking. With good attention it is often possible to discover some new thoughts and perhaps to surprise themselves. This effect is summed up by the phrase, 'I often don't know what I'm thinking until I've said it out loud'.

Because the listener knows that their turn for uninterrupted thinking time is coming shortly, they are able to suspend any urges to involve themselves with their partner's thinking by interrupting, asking for explanations or otherwise joining in.

Challenges
The method is simplicity itself. However it might present people with a challenge when this new method is first introduced to a group. It is so different from normal conversations and discussions with their interruptions and digressions that people can feel awkward with it. In this situation it is best to keep the time fairly short on the first few attempts to avoid too many silences and difficult empty spaces.

In my experience, it is usually better to pop in a short Think and Listen session, however brief, than to have people rush unprepared into discussion or decisions.

Other applications

The process is not only helpful in meetings. It can be used to good effect in many work settings. To clarify thoughts when writing reports, strategic planning and in any other circumstances where people may get stuck, are unable to think clearly or feel at a loss on how to proceed.

Some people find it beneficial to have a session prior to the start of work to off-load any matters that could pull their attention away from being fully present.

Think and Listen opportunities can have beneficial results at home, within families and between friends: People can be helpful to one another in preparing for making major decisions or having important conversations. Adults can help children to learn how to clarify their thoughts or be given opportunities to practice presentations.

Arguments and conflict may be averted if people can express their feelings out loud in the presence of an uninvolved and supportive person. A person's stress might be reduced or alleviated if he or she has a chance to talk about their situation in the presence of someone who is uninvolved, attentive and non-judgmental.

Taking a moment

Taking a moment to have a breather or create a pause can be useful to suggest at various times during a meeting. Whatever you call it this will allow everyone a moment to catch his or her breath, to settle down, to calm down, to relax or to think.

Benefits

Providing people with a space to breathe, to think, to pull themselves together, to get ready for the next thing, allows people to remain fully present with whatever's going on. This can prevent some of the activities that can get in the way of an effective meeting such as arguments, unclear thinking, hurried decisions or discord that prevents sensible decisions or, in some cases, any decision at all.

Challenges

Some people are uncomfortable with silence. Others mistakenly believe that an effective meeting is one that rushes through the agenda. As with an Opening Moment of Silence, these people may think that any pauses in the proceedings are a waste of time. Some people consider the use of a moment of silence to be 'flaky' and somehow not businesslike or professional. These people may need assuring that these moments of pause, of silence, are intelligent uses of time and are often the most efficient way of keeping a meeting on track and the participants fully engaged in the proceedings.

Applications

> At the end of one process to allow people a space in which to get ready for the next thing.

> In the middle of any heated exchange or confused discussion.

> To give people time to get to grips with information.

> To allow some time to consider a decision, before a vote, for example.

Instructions could be something like 'let's just take a moment to calm down... Let's take a minute to think about what is going on here... let's have pause before we decide upon this... let's take a moment to relax after all this activity/excitement... let's just take a bit of time after completing this item before we move on to the next.'

'Let's take a moment' could be your lifeline in tricky situations!

Communication processes
Constructive Communication

Constructive Communication is at the heart of my work and is a theme that runs through everything I do. Elements of what it means, how to be a constructive communicator and the difference that it can make appear throughout my writing. By following the simple guidelines below and modeling the suggested behavior, meeting managers can encourage participants to also communicate constructively. This could make a significant contribution to meetings being effective and enjoyable.

Constructive Listening

People are listening constructively when they show that their intention is to listen and understand. There are a number of ways they can do this:

> They stop what they are doing and give their undivided attention to the person who is speaking.

> They encourage people to fully express themselves.

> They listen with compassion and an open heart and mind: without interruption, judgment or criticism.

> They clarify anything they don't understand and check out that what they heard was what was actually said or meant.

> They make sure that people have said everything they need to say and have felt accurately heard and fully understood.

Constructive Speaking

This means speaking respectfully, clearly, directly, honestly, compassionately and supportively. People can do this by:

- Speaking respectfully to all people at all times.
- Saying what they mean and meaning what they say.
- Clearly stating their ideas, suggestions, opinions and conclusions.
- Honestly and respectfully expressing how they feel about any situation.
- Avoiding leaving things out, covering up emotions, pretending all is well or denying what it is that they want or need.
- Giving supportive feedback about what they observe.
- Speaking kindly and avoiding gossip.
- Being compassionate and avoiding making judgmental statements.
- Avoiding making criticisms unless constructive and supportive.

Making 'I' statements

By using 'I' statements people can avoid making generalizations and instead take ownership of their thoughts and ideas.

Generalization

It is quite common for people in meetings (and in most other situations for that matter) to speak in general terms instead of taking responsibility for their own opinions. They may say something like 'Everybody thinks that…' when they mean 'I think that…' 'People won't make changes like that' when they really mean 'I would find it difficult to make changes like that'.

Participants might talk generally about 'other people' or 'someone' or say 'you' or 'one' instead of 'I'. This may help them to feel less exposed to criticism or judgment and avoid having to justify their opinions or offer any explanations. However, these vague generalizations can get in the way of clarity and progress and can lead to uncertainty and mistrust within the group.

> When 'I' statements are used consistently, meetings will be dealing with information coming directly from the participants' own thoughts and experience.

Taking responsibility

There is a tendency amongst some people to mistakenly believe that 'I' statements are an indication of selfishness, self-centeredness or self-importance. 'I' statements are not about that; they are about taking personal responsibility. By prefixing what we say with the word 'I' we are taking responsibility for the statement we are making. 'I think... I feel... I wonder... I am concerned... I notice... I prefer... I would like...' are examples of ways for beginning sentences that show we take responsibility for our thoughts, feelings and actions.

Meetings in which people are requested to use 'I' statements to say clearly what they think, how they feel and what they really mean, become meetings based upon openness and honesty.

A greater sense of understanding can be achieved in meetings when participants are invited to share their perspective, their information, their experience and feelings about the topic under discussion. This can help other participants to understand the reasons for their opinion or concern.

In meetings in which participants 'own' their statements and stand clearly behind the views they express and the remarks they make, are meetings in which trust and mutual respect can develop and underpin the proceedings. The use of 'I' statements will go a long way to achieving these aims.

Preventing confrontation

The appropriate use of 'I' statements can be very effective means of communicating clearly in a non-confrontational, non-threatening manner. 'I have a different perspective on... I have a different experience... I have some misgivings... I can see other possibilities... I have another option to offer... I would like to hear other opinions... I would like us to explore more options...' are ways of challenging strong statements made by people without those people having to defend themselves or their points of view, which is what conflict is usually based upon.

By the way, 'I think you're an idiot' is not an appropriate 'I' statement! 'I think you are...' followed by any accusation, any unkind, uncomplimentary or insulting remark is an attack. Such attacks in meetings or anywhere else are unlikely to improve relationships, create harmony or reduce conflict. These sorts of attack can be avoided by the appropriate use of 'I' statements which describe thoughts and ideas, feelings and concerns in a responsible and respectful manner.

'I heard you say'

The simple, 'I heard you say...' process is based upon repeating back what a person has said. It is easy to use and can be helpful in clearing up misunderstandings and avoiding or resolving conflicts in many situations.

If two people are at loggerheads, it can be useful to introduce an 'I heard you say' process. After the first person has spoken, invite the second person to repeat back what they heard that person say. The roles are then reversed.

If a group is divided or polarized, a representative of each side could be invited to communicate their group's thoughts and feelings. A representative from the other side then repeats back what they just heard. The roles are then reversed.

In repeating what has been said, opposing views can often be better understood.

I have observed the mood of meetings change dramatically for the better after such exchanges.

Asking 'How does this help?'

When a person has made a remark or behaved in a meeting in a manner that is likely to be detrimental to the proceedings, the question could be asked of them: 'How does this help?'

It is vital that the tone of voice used in asking this question is one of respectful enquiry. It is essential that there is no trace of accusation, indignation or mockery in the voice as this is likely to inflame the situation instead of improving it.

Following a statement/suggestion/idea/request/criticism/behavior, etc., that feels detrimental to the meeting, ask 'How does this help:

- ➢ With this situation?
- ➢ To contribute to finding a workable solution?
- ➢ To support this person?
- ➢ To improve co-operation within the group?
- ➢ To encourage openness?
- ➢ To eliminate fear?
- ➢ To continue dialogue?
- ➢ To prevent conflict?
- ➢ Fit with the agreed values and ethics of this group?

And so on.

If the person can identify no benefits from their own behavior or remark then he or she can be requested to alter his or her behavior or restate the remark in a more appropriate way. For example, 'that's a stupid suggestion,' could be changed to, 'I have concerns and doubts about that suggestion'. This allows for these concerns and doubts to be explored in a non-confrontational way.

Benefits

This process requires people to take responsibility for their remarks and their behavior. It is a method for making clear that there is no place in the meeting for aggressive behavior, bullying or domineering tactics. And that judgments, criticisms and unkind remarks will be open to scrutiny by the group.

> Asking 'how does this help...?' is a way of challenging inappropriate behavior without accusing the person concerned. This could encourage people to be more respectful towards each other and to think before they speak.

Challenges

Most people are not used to being challenged about their behavior or the way in which they speak to people. This is especially the case with people who are used to dominating proceedings, to controlling situations, to getting their own way or speaking their mind - regardless of the feelings of others.

People may need to be assured that their concerns and opinions will be noted by the group and are more likely to be taken into consideration when presented in a more appropriate manner.

Reality check

Some people have a habit of speaking in general terms rather than owning their opinions or the statements they make. They might start their sentences by saying things like 'everybody thinks...' or 'nobody wants to...' instead of saying 'I think...' or 'I don't want to...' Sometimes people might express statements that they believe to be true, which can be surprising, disruptive, or distressing or seem to be at variance with the mood of the meeting.

People might voice their assumptions about how other people present perceive them. In these situations it can be useful to call for 'a Reality Check'.

Method

To check out with the other participants the reality of what someone has said, you might say to that person something like: 'Megan, I have just heard you make a statement that I feel would be useful for you to check out with the rest of the group/meeting. (You might need to repeat what you heard or ask the person to repeat what they said).

Then ask the group for 'a reality check'. Something along the lines of 'could we see a show of hands from those who agree with/share the same perspective as Megan?' Pause to count. 'Now those who disagree or have a different perspective raise your hand please'.

This method can also be used to help people understand that their behavior is creating difficulties or is unacceptable to the group. In which case the request for a reality check could be along the lines of 'John, even though we have all made agreements about being respectful to one another, I hear you making derogatory remarks about the things that some members are saying. I wonder if you realize the effect that your remarks are having on the group. I suggested we conduct a reality check on how your remarks are being received by them. Can we see a show of hands from those who feel uncomfortable/offended/upset by John's behavior? And now those who feel John's remarks are acceptable?

Although this method may appear to be confrontational, it is not intended as such, even though the person having their reality checked might feel embarrassed by the outcome. Nor is it intended to make people out to be wrong, bad or stupid. The intention of this process is to provide participants with the opportunity of seeing how the others are receiving their communication or are affected by their behavior. It gives those in the meeting the responsibility for managing their reactions and prevents undercurrents of discontent or disapproval.

> As it puts individuals on the spot this process ought, where possible, to be used only after other methods have been tried, such as reminding participants of agreements made.

Calling attention

This is alerting the participants' attention to what is really happening when discussions become heated, when conflict is brewing or when everyone wants to talk and no one wants to listen.

It is used to draw attention away from the content of what is being said and focusing on the process of communication or interaction. For example, you might say, 'I am finding it difficult to follow these arguments when so many people are talking at the same time. I know there are people wanting to offer good ideas and share their experience, and I would like to be able to hear them clearly and without disruption.' This approach indicates to all those present that the heated style of the exchange is unhelpful without attacking anyone's ideas or position.

Calling attention is also a good strategy to use to counter many of the most common blocking or disrupting tactics in meetings. It can be used to identify such things as defeatism, pessimism, manipulation and bullying. It can short-circuit arguments and the time wasting behavior of axe-grinding and storytelling.

Having a Quiet Word

Having a Quiet Word with someone whose behavior is upsetting to the group is usually more effective in the long term than having an argument or making demands of them.

A Quiet Word needs to be just that - quiet. This type of conversation is to be held in private and out of the hearing of anyone else. It is best conducted as soon as possible after the person has spoken or acted in a way that is inappropriate or upsetting. However, in most meeting situations the Quiet Word may need to be delayed until the end of the event.

There is much more information on Constructive Communication in SMART TALKING and SMART LISTENING in the YOU MAKE THE DIFFERENCE series that are available in paperback and e-book format from Amazon and accessible through our website:
www.youmakethedifference.net

Processes for sharing information

Paired sharing

Participants pair up to discuss a topic or an aspect of an issue and bring the results of their conversation back to share with the group. Through discussion and questions each pair can widen their perspective and deepen their understanding of the topic.

Each pair might choose their topic because they share a common interest in or knowledge of it. Or each pair could be given their topic by the meeting manager or select it randomly through some process such as picking out of a bowl pieces of paper on which topics or aspects of the topic are written.

Benefits

Through this process the consideration of a variety of aspects of an issue can take place simultaneously. The findings of each pair can then inform the wider thinking of the whole group. Or a paired sharing can give participants in a large meeting an opportunity to share thoughts and ideas about the issue in hand with one other person. A synopsis of a number of these discussions could be shared with the whole group at the end of this process.

Popcorn

This is an alternative to a Go-Round for sharing within the circle. There may be times when people need to carefully consider what they say before speaking; especially about things that are sensitive or about which they feel deeply. Instead of people speaking in order around the circle they might prefer to speak when they feel ready or feel moved to do so.

Applications
When sensitive issues are being discussed or when the whole objective of the meeting is to hear in depth what participants think and feel about an issue.

Benefits
People speak when it works best for them to do so. Having had some time to think they might then speak with greater clarity or offer more information.

Challenges
Keeping track of who has spoken can take some vigilance, especially in large groups. It is important to check that everyone has had his or her turn before ending the session.

Popcorn can take considerably longer than a Go-Round because the gaps between speakers will be longer as participants wait to make sure there is space for them to speak or they are not about to interrupt someone or be interrupted by someone as they start to speak.

There are some people who wish to be the last person to speak. This might be because of shyness, of reticence to speak, or the desire to be the most memorable participant. If there is more than one person in the group with the intention of speaking last then the final stages of the process can drag on as they each wait for the other to go first. Some intervention may be necessary to alleviate this.

Talking stick

> This method has been used in meetings by tribal peoples for perhaps thousands of years to ensure that the person speaking is the focus of attention of the group.

The Talking Stick is placed in the centre of the circle where it will be picked up and held by each person who is moved to speak. That person holds the stick until they have completed what they have to say then they replace the stick in the centre. During the time that any person holds the stick they are givien uninterrupted, respectful attention by all of those present.

The Talking Stick could be a simple piece of wood or it might be elaborately decorated. However, it doesn't actually have to be a stick. I have seen a number of items used: stones, large pebbles (painted or otherwise), crystals and other items that have significance for a particular group of people.

The Talking Stick, whatever its nature, might be found or created specifically for a particular event or the same one could be used each time a group meets. I have participated in annual gatherings and events where the same decorated talking sticks are brought year after year. Many facilitators bring their own Talking Stick to meetings or events.

Asking questions

The meeting manager's role is to guide participants through processes by asking questions.

Open Questions

Apart from a very few situations it is wise to avoid asking closed questions. Closed questions are ones to which the answer is likely to be limited to: 'yes' or 'no' or 'maybe'. Instead, always ask open questions; those that need to be answered with more than that.

> I remember an old rhyme about asking for information:
> 'At my service I have five good men and true:
> Mr. Why, Mr. What, Mr. Where, Mr. When, and Mr. Who.'

Open questions usually begin with one of these words such as, 'What needs to happen in order to...?' Where would this...?' How could we...? 'When might it...?

However, I caution against using Mr. Why. 'Why' is a word that can give a question a feeling of an interrogation. The 'Why' word might trigger a reaction in some people for whom it may bring back memories or the feelings associated with being questioned in a critical or judgmental manner by parents, teachers or others authority figures.

Sample Questions

Data and information gathering questions:

What do you remember?
What grabbed your attention?
What did you hear people saying?
What did you hear?
What did you see?
What did you do?
What procedures were followed?

Sometimes these questions will need to be very specific:

How many volunteer hours were offered to us last month?
How many people use the service each week?

How many projects were run over the summer?
What was the most successful fundraiser last year?

Probing questions

What does that mean?
How does this…?
What might happen if…?
What would it take to…?
How would it be if…?
What could you do to…?
When will you…?
How will we recognize when…?

Interpretive questions

What are the key images?
What are your key insights?
What did you learn?
What have you learned about yourself?
How does this relate to your situation?
How does this compare to previous situations?
What are the key ideas or messages to take away?
What does this mean to you?
What impact could this have on your work/situation/life?

Decision and action questions

What changes will you/we need to make?
What will you/we need to do differently?
What will be the first steps?
What needs to happen from here?
How can you/we improve your/our performance?
How can you/we apply what you/we have learned?

Reflective questions

How did you react at that moment?
How did you feel when the activity was completed?
What concerns do/did you have?

Debriefing and Evaluation Questions

What did you like about the event?
What did not work well for you?
What got you excited?
When were you frustrated?
What could be improved upon?

What was the highlight of the event?

There are of course many variations of these questions and many others you could ask.

Be creative with your questions to maintain interest, enthusiasm and focus.

Processes for gathering and working with ideas

There are many ways of gathering ideas and suggestions in meetings and events. Go-Rounds give people in smaller meetings the opportunity to express their ideas or concerns. Think and Listen sessions and Paired Sharing can be useful in clarifying thoughts prior to a Go-Round.

Short presentations can bring issues to the attention of the meeting participants. If the need is to generate ideas for discussion or action then a Brainstorming session may be the quickest and most effective process to use.

Brainstorming

Brainstorming is a tried and trusted way to gather a lot of ideas in a short space of time. It is useful for identifying information and for quickly generating a list of options, ideas, suggestions, problems, issues, opportunities, solutions, activities, topics for discussion, items for an agenda and so on.

Offering people the chance to free their thinking may produce a rich vein of options and suggestions. By involving all participants it can capture the full spectrum of group knowledge and creativity.

Brainstorming can be a helpful way to encourage reticent people to feel comfortable to offer their wisdom and put forward their ideas and wishes.

Care needs to be taken in preventing a Brainstorming session from being hijacked, swayed or unduly influenced by people with hidden or not so hidden, agendas. When status, money or politics are involved people can behave in a less than open manner. People in Brainstorming sessions have been known to have the intention to:

a.   Steer the Brainstorming in a particular direction.

b.   Manipulate people into believing that they had a say in a decision already made.

c.   Gain useful ideas in a manner that avoids having to give credit to the people who came up with them.

49

Brainstorming session
Step one

Choose or name the issue, topic or problem that needs to be addressed or for which ideas, solutions or options for action need to be found. Ask the most useful and incisive focusing questions that could engage the interest of most participants and that would move the meeting towards its goal. This could be as simple as asking for items for the Open Agenda or as wide-ranging as suggestions for projects or actions, which the group, organization or community could initiate or become involved in.

Step two

Invite the participants to come up with and shout out all the suggestions that come to mind regarding the topic.

➤ Ask easily answerable questions.

➤ Ask participants to state their ideas clearly and concisely using single word or short sentence descriptions.

➤ Give examples to help free their imagination, if necessary.

➤ Encourage the use of tangible statements for example 'something you can do, see or touch'.

➤ Ask participants to avoid intangible statement such 'feeling happy'.

Have someone write down every contribution on a flip chart or whiteboard.

Encourage all suggestions and solutions, no matter how imaginative, outrageous or impossible these ideas seem. The goal at this stage is to achieve quantity not quality. At this stage criticism of any suggestion is to be discouraged.

Continue until there is a decent list of suggestions or until the flow of ideas dries up.

> With a shy or reticent group, you may need to make a couple of contributions to the brainstorming session yourself to encourage the flow. These ought to be in question form: 'What about...?' 'Might this include...?' However, it will be empowering to the participants for you to withhold your suggestions until the participants have all expressed theirs.

As the facilitator it will usually be your role to facilitate their choices rather than contribute your own. Hold on to your own ideas unless the process is not flowing or producing many items. Provide prompts or ask questions only when necessary or where appropriate.

Give people time to respond – the analytical and amiable may need a bit longer than others. Get used to the silent gap, as people are thinking of how to best express their ideas. When the flow seems to have stopped, ask for any other ideas or ask: 'is there anyone else?' whilst looking at the general direction of those who have not been contributing.

Brainstorming is a highly energetic session. When people have no more answers to give, move on.

Step three

Invite the group to go through the list of suggestions and filter out or discount those that are wildly extreme or obviously inappropriate for the budget, the timescale or are unlikely to work for some reason. (These ought to be recorded anyway and kept for the time when restrictions such as inadequate budgets or other limitations might change).

Step four

How the items identified are now worked with will depend upon whether the object of the exercise is to collect workable items, widen the thinking or focusing the attention of the group.

Combining some of the ideas and topics can have several results. On the one hand, this might improve efficiency as these items may be aspects of the same issue and might possibly be dealt with together. On the other hand, bringing several thoughts or ideas together could broaden the scope of that topic. In grouping good ideas together further improved ones might be created. Not all items need to be grouped of course. Many will be stand-alone items.

Ask participants to identify if there are ideas that are related, have similar intent or have something in common. Form clusters of ideas or points of commonality. This is an important step in the Brainstorming process when the object of the exercise is to generate topics of discussion. It is especially valuable if this is a process to identify topics for an Open Agenda. This step shows the size of a topic and can indicate the amount of time likely to be required for addressing it.

Combining or connecting items may create new relationships between ideas. This can be useful if the purpose is to open up lateral or 'out of the box' thinking. Forming new relationships between topics can lead to exciting innovation and new concepts. Seemingly unrelated problems or challenges can be combined for the mutual benefit of all concerned.

For example:

This kind of thinking led to some residents of retirement villages becoming volunteer reading mentors to children in remedial reading programs in some New Zealand schools. For a few hours each week the retirees had something interesting and useful to do with their time with others than just people of their own age. The children benefited from the support of people who had experience, time and patience. Both groups benefited from these interactions and enjoyable relationships developed, especially amongst those whose own grandparents or grandchildren lived far away.

Step five

If the Brainstorming session so far has generated lots of ideas these need to be ranked or prioritized in order of importance, relevance or running order. There may be too many items to deal with at one meeting so it may be a challenge to get the group to identify and focus on the most important items or those appropriate for dealing with immediately.

Ways to prioritize/rank ideas.

A. Voting

As each item is indicated the participants vote for the one they consider the most important item by raising their hand. The item that receives the greatest number of votes is ranked first. Then further rounds of voting will be needed to rank the other items.

B. Labeling

This may be a good time to bring a fun element to the proceedings.

Give participants a variety of colored sticky dots and ask them to place one beside each of the items they consider most important. For example, place green for most important, blue for second, yellow for third and red for least valuable. Add up the colors for each item. Alternatively, the items could be awarded points. Participants write the number 10 next to the item they feel particularly passionate or strongly about and then rank other items in order of preference. Add up the numbers.

C. The Barometer

With chalk draw a line or an image of a barometer on the floor and point out which end is 'hot' in which end is 'cold'. Working through each item in turn, invite the participants to place themselves somewhere on the barometer that indicates their level of keenness to deal with the topic. If they think an issue is very hot they stand right at the hot end of the scale; if they have little interest they stand at the cold end or anywhere in between. This process gets people out of their chairs and moving around.

> The Barometer is also a useful process for gauging the mood of a meeting or carrying out a reality check. The end points of the continuum can be anything:
> Important – not important
> Practical – not practical
> Excellent idea – poor idea
> On the button – off track
> Etc..

The Barometer can also be used in assessing the impact of a talk, a presentation or discussion. In this case, people are invited to stand somewhere on the barometer before the talk, presentation or discussion to indicate their current opinion and then again afterwards to show if their view has changed.

Many of these processes can also be used in the Review and Evaluation at the end of meetings.

Alternative Brainstorming process

In facilitated meetings of large numbers of people, especially when an issue is complex, Brainstorming sessions could be handled in another way.

Participants could be divided into smaller groups, perhaps with a leader or spokesperson. In response to the focus questions the members of these groups write their ideas and suggestions on small post-it notes and stick them on to their group's board or flipchart. They can then group these into areas of similarity. The participants can decide upon a statement that sums up the essence of each of these groupings, which can then be filtered, ranked or prioritized by that group.

This separate group investigation works well when time is limited and a number of aspects of an issue need to be considered. This method could also be used to avoid confrontation when several groups have differing opinions or needs regarding an issue.

Processes for creating equal opportunities

It is vital for all participants to have equal opportunities to make their contribution to the meetings that they have taken the time to attend.

The Two-minute Rule

The two-minute rule is designed to create equal opportunities for people to speak. This is also useful for keeping meetings moving forward:

➢ It gives everyone an equal amount of time to have his or her say.

➢ Two minutes per person in a Go-Round allows sufficient time for individuals to introduce themselves or express their opinion on a topic.

➢ It allows sufficient time for individuals to make concise presentations.

Although some people will not use up the full two minutes, invoking the two-minute rule can help to estimate the length of time a process such as a Go-Round will take.

After one and a half minutes has elapsed of a person's turn you inform them that they have 30 seconds remaining.

Some participants may just be getting into their stride after two minutes and so might be difficult to stop. If people do not respond quickly to being told their time is up you may find it useful or necessary to ring a bell, ding a chime or blow a whistle.

No one speaks twice...

No one speaks twice until everyone has had the opportunity to speak once.

In some meetings there may be a strong cultural conditioning at work that insists that discussion is equivalent to the freedom to ruminate out loud or to shout down opposite views. Discussions can turn into a free for all where anybody can say whatever they like and for as long as they like. Without structure, discussions commonly create problems such as arguments and exclusion, polarization and dominant behavior. Often in these conditions of competition, good thinking goes out the window and little gets done. Nothing is quite so likely to prevent people from enjoying a meeting than the development of an all-out argument or a two-person, points scoring conflict.

The process

The meeting manager proposes the guideline, 'no one speaks twice until everyone has had the opportunity to speak once'. A co-facilitator, scribe or recorder might be asked to take charge of monitoring who has spoken, leaving the meeting manager free to manage the process, watch the group for signs of aggression or the under engagement of some participants, and find ways of encouraging the reticent to speak.

Benefits

This method can be adapted after a while – 'now, no one to speak three times until everyone has had a chance to speak twice', and then, if necessary, 'any more for any more?'

This method works by eliminating the possibility for everyone to command the airtime by speaking several times in quick succession. This process can be used to bring structure to discussions. It is particularly useful when there is the possibility of arguments developing or where certain group members tend to dominate proceedings. It is not possible to create an argument, for example, if there is no opportunity for a dingdong type of transaction to develop.

Managing contributions to discussions through the use of this method also ensures that there is a sufficient space to encourage shy people to contribute, or for discussions to be refreshingly short and to the point.

> No one speaks twice... also works to eliminate the unnecessary trivia and irrelevances that can often fill up meeting time.

Challenges

Being told that 'No one speaks twice...' can upset people who cherish battles of wits. Some people believe that conflict sharpens thinking and that a good argument precedes a good decision. This approach is generally much less useful than people imagine.

This process can be especially difficult to use in established groups or those with lots of strong-minded people. If there is resistance to using this method or it doesn't seem easy to introduce it then seek to use it without being explicit. For example, when a participant is about to speak for the second or third time and shutting out others by doing so you might say something like: 'before we hear from you again let's see if anyone else who has not yet spoken would like to say something'.

In this naturalized form it is a skill often used by chairpersons in conventional meetings. However, not being able to name the method does mean that it remains relatively obscure.

Decision-making procedures and processes

Decision-making in well-managed, inclusive meetings ought to be easy and straightforward. Through discussion and appropriate processes, choices usually become obvious and solutions will often present themselves.

Doubts about debates

Debating is a traditional method of bringing into the open the pros and cons of a topic. Because debating is intended to result in a winner and a loser it is often adversarial and can become acrimonious. I doubt that there is a place for debate in inclusive meetings.

Instead, the various aspects of or opinions on a topic could be presented and questions posed and answered without any need to resort to criticism or attack opposing views. The participants can then make up their minds and vote accordingly.

Clarifying and Summarizing

The ability to clarify and succinctly summarize are important skills in meeting management. They are used to identify common themes that link thoughts that have been expressed, and can help organize a group's ideas and support them to develop solutions. They are vital components in assisting voting procedures.

It is essential to be concise when summarizing to avoid waffling or going into unnecessary detail.

Voting

When a decision to be voted upon has been clearly identified and summarized there are a number of voting procedures that can be used. These are best kept as simple and uncomplicated as possible.

Hands up

People are asked to put up their hand to vote for or against the proposal.

Stand up and be counted

People stand up to vote for or against the proposal.

Either end

'Yes' and 'no' ends of the room are identified and people move to stand where they wish to place their vote.

Passing through

This is similar to the parliamentary process where people choose a 'yes' or 'no' point in the room to pass through to be counted.

Green for go

People are given green and red cards and asked to hold up a green card for a 'yes' vote and a red card for a 'no' vote.

Color Swatch

This is an advanced form of the previous method.

I first came across this in the mid-1990s when I volunteered to support a World Summit of Children. This conference was attended by young people between the ages of 14 and 18, who, representing dozens of countries, had gathered together to review the Convention on the Rights of the Child and explore how this was being implemented around the world. This remains one of my most inspiring experiences.

When encouraged to manage their own conference - that is when adults could be persuaded to resist the temptation to 'help' (meddle) - these youngsters devised efficient and creative meeting methods, processes and procedures to support their interactions.

The color swatch is one of several of these methods I have used on many occasions since.

This method is most suitable for smaller meetings such as committee, departmental, board or trustee meetings.

Creating Color Swatches

For each swatch, five different colored cards are cut into strips of around 6x16cm.

Suggested color choices:

> ➤ A green card for 'I accept' or 'yes'.
> ➤ A red card for 'I do not accept' or 'no'.
> ➤ A yellow for 'I don't know' or 'abstaining'.
> ➤ A white card indicates 'I have a question'.
> ➤ A black card suggests that the person who is speaking is 'getting off track'.

To avoid any misunderstandings, the appropriate words can be written on each card in large letters with a black felt marker. If the card has two purposes such as 'I don't know' and 'abstaining', these can be written on a different side of the yellow card.

A hole can then be punched in one end of the cards, which are then threaded onto a ring (the sort found on a key ring). This keeps the cards together and makes it easy to find and hold up a required card at the appropriate time. If the color swatches are to be used regularly they ought to be laminated.

There needs to be a Color Swatch for each participant in the meeting, including the meeting manager if he or she has a vote. Otherwise, a black card for Off-Track and a white card for I have a question, will be sufficient for them.

People such as committee members or those who attend regular group meetings could keep their Color Swatch to bring to the meetings. Many people personalize their Color Swatch in some way, such as with a nametag or whatever came on the key ring.

The Color Swatch method is not only an efficient way of counting votes and testing the mood of a meeting it can be a valuable aid to a meeting manager as each card held up clearly indicates the participant's intention.

Benefits

This is a clear and quick method. Supports proxy voting if spare cards are available for the proxy votes.

Challenges

Cards can be mislaid. Traditionalists might resist such a 'new-fangled' procedure.

Balloting

Balloting is probably most appropriate for elections when there is a choice of a number of candidates or when the election takes place outside of a meeting.

> Transparency is an important element in inclusive meetings. If a need is felt for a secret ballot on some issue during a meeting this would suggest that more work needs to be done on building trust or eradicating fear within the group.

Majority vote

The method most commonly used for arriving at a decision is through a majority vote. It will first be necessary to establish what percentage of those present constitutes the majority. This may vary from 60% to 90%, although around 75% is most common. In my experience this is an occasion where the 80/20 rule can be usefully employed, as 80% clearly is the majority. Determining 80% of those present is an easy calculation.

A loyal minority

When a decision is reached by a majority of people, there is sometimes a tendency amongst the remaining minority to be disgruntled about the decision and to be disruptive in some way. This can be anything from persistent grumbling about the decision; to actively attempting to undermine it. To avoid this, an important part of the majority voting process is to request those who are in disagreement with the decision to be recognized as a loyal minority.

These people ought to have been given ample opportunity to express their opinion before the vote was taken and so everyone present can be aware of their concerns. After the decision is made these concerns can be acknowledged by the meeting manager with a request for a commitment from those people to be loyal to the group by resisting any temptation to chip away at the decision through criticism or negative judgments or to desist from any action that could undermine the implementation of the decision. Each of these participants ought to be encouraged to make this commitment verbally. They ought then to be appreciated for their willingness to be supportive of the majority choice.

If those people fail to keep to their commitment at any time during the period the decision is being implemented they could be reminded of their commitment to be loyal to the group.

If, at some stage in the future, the concerns of this minority prove to be accurate, then their foresight ought to be acknowledged and appreciated.

Creating Consensus

> The ideal method for a group to reach a decision is through consensus.

Full consensus is achieved when everyone present agrees upon a decision. In order to reach this point work may need to be done on clarifying and refining the proposal. Sub issues or different facets of the topic can muddy the waters and bog down process. Dealing with these effectively is vital to consensus.

To reach consensus there are a number of things to bear in mind:

a. The more contentious the issue the more difficult it usually is to reach consensus.

b. The greater the number of people involved in the decision the more difficult it is likely to be to reach consensus.

c. Reaching full consensus can be a lengthy process requiring patience, commitment, and clear, honest communication from everyone involved.

d. The greater the number of people involved in the decision the longer it is likely to take to reach consensus.

e. Arriving at consensus on an important or contentious issue might take several meetings. If any of the factors in these meetings are changed, such as people leaving the process or new people coming into it, the process is likely to be prolonged.

Reaching consensus
Phase 1
The issue upon which consensus is to be achieved needs to be clearly stated.
Phase 2
Those of differing opinions gather into groups of like-minded people. For example those who would intend to vote 'yes' collect into one group, those who would vote 'no' gather into another and those who are undecided gather into a third group.
Phase 3
Each group comes up with clear statements of their reasons for their opinion and chooses one or in the case of large groups two representatives to present these.
Phase 4
These representatives meet in the centre of the room, where, they are facilitated, in full view of everyone, to put forward their group's views and opinions about the topic and the reasons for their group's current decision.

Phase 5

The representatives then return to their groups, which discuss whether or not what they have heard from other groups has influenced their group's current decision. It is possible that having a clearer understanding of other people's perspective helps a consensus decision to be reached at this point. If not, each group discusses what they have heard and then comes up with a proposal that could help a move towards consensus. For example the 'no' or 'don't know' group might come up with a statement something like 'we could move closer to agreement if...' they then state their new proposal. The 'yes' group could make a proposal that accommodates some of the wishes or concerns of the other two groups.

Phase 6

The representatives return to the centre of the room and offer their group's proposals or new thinking. They then go back to their groups where the new proposals and ideas heard from the other groups are considered. It is possible that consensus may be reached at this point if concerns or requests have been accommodated satisfactory.

This process continues with the representatives going backwards and forwards to communicate their group's evolving thinking or their suggested adjustments to the proposal. Consensus is reached when everyone in the room can agree. This method of reaching consensus usually requires compromises to be made by each group.

The groups might have their discussions in separate rooms with only their representatives having a full sense of the overall picture. However, this can add to the existing feelings of separation created by the differing opinions and is likely to prevent the meeting from being fully inclusive. When all of the groups occupy areas of the same room for their discussions this allows the whole of the process to be transparent and to create a sense of 'we are all in this together'.

> To reach a necessary or urgent decision within a time scale, an agreement could already have been made to switch to majority voting as a last resort if consensus cannot be achieved within the allocated time. In these circumstances it is especially important to fully recognize the concerns of those unwilling to agree to consensus and to establish them as a committed Loyal Minority Group for which they ought to be acknowledged.

One step further

There is a further step that can be taken towards reaching consensus that was demonstrated in a consensus decision-making training run by my friend Robin Shohet:

We trainees were invited to pair up with someone of around an equal size to ourselves. We were then asked to arm-wrestle with each other. As expected, the strongest of each pair won.

We were then asked to each think of an ideal outcome to some personal or global difficulty and to share that with our partner. We were to imagine that whoever in the pair won the next bout of arm wrestling could magically achieve their desired outcome. Even though we each passionately pleaded our cause to our 'opponents', in the hope of eliciting their understanding and support, in most cases, although not all, the strongest person in each pair won again.

Robin and a participant then prepared to arm-wrestle one another. Robin said his ideal outcome was world peace and the participant's was the eradication of global poverty. The winner of this seemed to be a foregone conclusion as one man was two meters tall and strongly built, while the other was of much shorter and lighter stature. The bout took only two seconds. First, Robin pushed the participant's arm down onto the table and then immediately the participant whipped Robin's arm over and pinned it to the table on the other side. It was immediately clear that both men were attempting to allow the other to succeed!

Robin then explained that in this pre-arranged demonstration he had approached the arm wrestling bout with the intention of wanting the other person to achieve his desired outcome. The participant explained that he had had the same intention regarding Robin.

Of course, this was so obvious. Why would this person not want Robin to achieve his ideal of world peace? Why would Robin not want him to have his ideal outcome of the eradication of poverty?

This only required a small shift from 'To get what I want I have to stop you from getting what you want' to 'how can I help you to get what you want?' From 'one of us has to lose for the other to win'; to 'how can we help each other to get our needs met?' This was all so simple! And yet it changed everything!

This simple shift of intention from needing to win to wanting to find an agreement where others also achieve their goals or fulfill their needs expands thinking, frees up creativity, and engages our compassion and care.

This small step of changing intention can be a giant leap in decision-making.

When hearing this process described, some people say, 'Yes but this doesn't make any sense, nobody wins!' On the contrary, if my intention is for you to achieve your goals and I have done whatever I can to bring that about, I will gain a sense of accomplishment. So will you, if you have done the same for me. This is Win, Win!

Another statement that is sometimes made about this process is, 'What if two groups of people want totally opposite results, or for one group to get what they want means that it is detrimental to the other group?' In my experience, most situations, especially those in organizations or within communities are rarely so polarized. There are usually enough areas of common ground upon which some form of agreement can be made.

This process is similar to some that are used to deal with serious conflict. If this process can be successfully employed to resolve life threatening, conflict situations around the world, it can surely be helpful within group, organizational or community situations. I have not yet experienced any everyday situation that could not be resolved to the sufficient satisfaction of two seemingly opposing needs. There is usually enough common ground or mutual need that can be built upon to reach a workable solution, even if that might require continuous monitoring.

Another concern expressed is 'Yes but, what if I behave generously and make a decision to help others to get what they want and then they don't do the same for me?' My usual reply is, 'so what? What was your real intention? Did you genuinely intend for that person to get what they needed? If so, that ought not to be affected by anything that happens to you. You made your choice and they made theirs.' Just because somebody might not behave in the manner that we would like, that ought not to prevent us from behaving in the way that we believe to be right.

> We each face choices small and large every minute of the day. Many of these choices are whether to be part of a problem or part of a solution. For we human beings to evolve into a species of mutually supportive, compassionate people, requires us to choose to become part of the solutions rather than be part of the problems. We can each choose to do the very best we can in this regard in every situation.

Making a quantum shift

My understanding of a quantum shift is when a tiny change made in something results in a whole new outcome of enormous potential.

What kind of society could we have if whenever people wanted different outcomes each of them became intent on supporting the other to achieve their desired outcomes?

What changes in our attitudes, our thinking and our decision-making would be required when we want those with whom we are in discussion or disagreement to get what they need?

Would it require us to have greater understanding of people? Would it require us to see past our own needs to the needs of others and the reason for their desired outcomes? Would this require us to see people as having value equal to that of our own?

Perhaps this small change in each of us in the focus of our attention from 'me' to 'we' is all that is needed to make the Paradigm Shift from a world in which we compete with one another for everything; into a world of genuine cooperation towards global sustainability.

Processes for ending meetings

Reflection and review, agreeing next steps, summarizing, evaluation and feedback are some of the usual components of the final stages of meetings. To omit any of these when they are necessary might result in the loss of useful information and leave participants feeling incomplete with the meeting.

This is when the group needs to make a balanced assessment of its achievements and its progress. Implementing a process that includes a summing up of the achievements, a reflection upon the learning from the processes, the interactions between the participants and a restating of next steps and agreed commitments ensures that progress, learning, realizations and gains are not lost.

Meetings will have begun with the outlining of the purpose. During the event, methods will have been initiated through which people could engage with that purpose. Now is the time to look at what has been achieved, to acknowledge the effort involved in getting there, and look ahead to next steps.

Reflection and review

Reflect upon the achievements

Ask questions such as, 'What is the most important achievement to come out of this meeting?' 'Name some other achievements from today that will further the aims of the group/help achieve the meeting purpose?'

Reflect upon the next steps

Ask questions such as:

> 'What steps are now going to be taken to fulfill this purpose?'
> 'What contribution will each of you now make towards fulfilling the agreements that have come out of this meeting?'
> 'What will you do differently from now on?'
> 'What changes will you now make as a result of what you've learned today?'
> 'What steps are you going to take as a result of this meeting?'
> 'How will we recognize when those changes have been made?'

These questions can bring further clarity and may provide an obvious forward direction. They can also assist in reinforcing key elements of an agenda item. They can encourage commitment to action!

Reflect on the processes

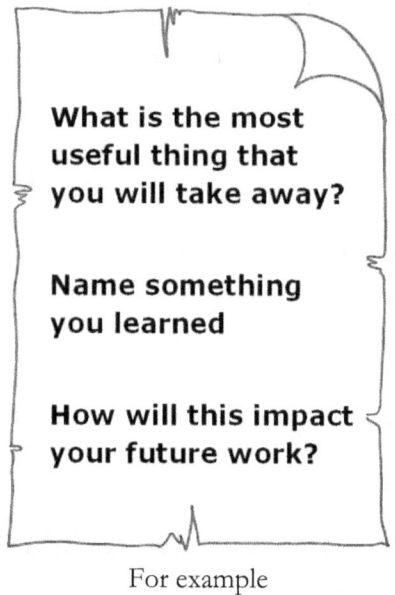

What is the most useful thing that you will take away?

Name something you learned

How will this impact your future work?

For example

Reflect upon the interactions

Enquire, 'what has been most enjoyable in the process of working together? What has been difficult? What is one thing we need to pay more attention to the next time we are together?' Asking for a single word to describe a process or the meeting can be a quick and revealing contribution.

The number of questions can be varied depending in what circumstances they will be answered and upon the number of people present. In small meetings each person can answer these questions in one Go-Round. In larger events, these could be considered in small home or stakeholder groups. In some large events or if time is getting short these questions can be answered in a paired sharing. A selection of these could be then shared with the whole group at the end of the process.

Summarizing, Evaluation and Feedback

Summarizing

> The ability to succinctly summarize what has taken place and been decided upon is an essential skill in meeting management.

Be concise when summarizing to avoid waffling or going into unnecessary detail. Part of a meeting manager's role is to support the maintenance of the purposefulness of the group beyond the end of a meeting. Closing with a sense of achieved purpose is an essential aspect of any meeting.

Evaluation

Example questions to prompt evaluation would be:
> ➤ What worked well/what did you most enjoy in the meeting?
> ➤ What could have been done better?
> ➤ How well did it meet your expectations?
> ➤ What would you like to see included in the next meeting?

An important part of this evaluation and feedback will be about the way in which the meeting was managed.

Questionnaires

A common practice is for the use of questionnaires as review, evaluation and feedback methods. This written form may be a requirement by those to whom the group is accountable or to be used as a way to follow-up on decisions and actions. Have a practice run to trial the questionnaire to ensure that it makes sense and will provide the key information required.

Because questionnaires need to be written, reproduced, handed out, collected in, read and probably filed away, questionnaire seem to be less than desirable in inclusive and self-contained meetings.

Sometimes questionnaires require no signature and so participants might use this anonymity for making criticism. This may be the only way to receive the required information. On the other hand it may be a lost opportunity. Verbal evaluation allows people to speak out and take responsibility for what they say and for all participants to hear perspectives that may be similar to or quite different from their own.

Feedback
Verbal

In most conventional meetings it is not customary for participants to give direct verbal feedback to people who have managed the meeting. The feedback is likely to be there however. It may be indirect, showing up as difficult or disruptive behavior, a sense of dissatisfaction or a lack of commitment to actions, all of which are difficult for meeting managers to interpret.

Direct verbal feedback is an important source of information for meeting managers. It enables them to learn about the quality and effectiveness of their meeting designs as perceived by the participants. Requesting 'I' statement responses encourages the participants to take responsibility for their feedback and more ownership of the meeting.

The review, evaluation and feedback of the meeting can be handled verbally in a number of ways: In a Go-Round in the whole group; in small home or stakeholder groups-a spokesperson from each gives a synopsis of these to the whole group; in Paired Sharing or Think and Listen sessions where some examples are shared with the whole group.

Active evaluation and feedback

There might be a need for some more active processes for these, particularly when energy may be at a low-ebb at the end of the day or a long meeting. Instead of asking for written or verbal responses to the focusing questions the use of one or more of the active responses that have elements of fun attached might be beneficial. Most of the processes such as labeling, numbering or barometer already listed under Ranking in the Brainstorming section could be good for this.

Meeting manager's self-assessment

We can all benefit from reviewing our own performance. You could do your own quick self-assessment of your role in the meeting while the participants are doing their review and evaluation.

Ask yourself:
 a. What did I do well?
 b. What could I have done different?
 c. What have I learned?

You could then share this self-assessment with the group during the feedback session and, if you wish, ask for a reality check from them. 'I feel we could have benefited from spending more time on...' 'I think that the new icebreaker I used was effective and enjoyable' 'I'm not sure if my directions on the... process were clear enough, etc. Can I have a reality check please?' This assessment can be brought into any Debrief process with co-facilitators or support person.

Debriefing

Perhaps the idea of going over a meeting again, either in your mind or with others, might make your heart sink. And yet, a lot can be gained from debriefing:

a. What was learned?
b. What worked?
c. What did not?
d. What did I/you/we do well?
e. What could be improved upon for future meetings?
f. How might that be achieved?

If you managed the meeting with co-facilitators you will want to do this together. If other group members fulfilled some function during the meeting they will benefit from debriefing their part.

If you managed the meeting alone it could be beneficial to pre-arrange with a participant or some support person to debrief with you.

Have compassion for yourself

There may be occasions when you are less than happy with a meeting, feel dissatisfied in the way you handled it or disappointed with an outcome. Have compassion for yourself as you debrief what happened. Remember to appreciate yourself for the things you did well and not to dwell entirely upon the things you might have done better. Appreciate yourself for your willingness to manage the meeting, especially if this was a voluntary activity.

Continue those feelings of compassion and self-appreciation as you replenish yourself during the period immediately after your meetings. Choose a form of self-replenishment that works best for you and your circumstances. Take a short break, close your eyes for a few minutes, slowly sip some water or a calming beverage, go outside for some deep breaths of fresh air, have a few minutes' walk, have a quiet, mind-calming meditation.

When experiencing exhaustion or frustration after a difficult or trying meeting it is wise to acknowledge those feelings rather than ignore them and hope they will go away. It would be sensible to avoid, whenever possible, immediately commencing another meeting or any situation that might be stressful or difficult. It would be prudent to avoid driving immediately, especially in the dark, in bad weather or in heavy traffic. It could be smart to avoid drinking alcohol or using other substances as a way of blocking out or forgetting what has just happened. A calming cup of green or herbal tea or hot chocolate could be far more beneficial.

> If you are feeling less than happy with the interactions or the outcomes of a meeting/event it can be helpful to remember that you did the very best you could do at the time.

3

GROUP GAMES

Games can be used to good effect in many meetings and events. They provide easy opportunities for people to make connection with one another, to have experience of cooperating together and to develop trust within the group.

To ensure that these games are fully inclusive they can be tailored for specific requirements and most can be adapted to fit the capacities of all the participants.

Ice Breaking and Introduction Games

Many workshops and meetings, especially among strangers, large gatherings or long events such as conferences can benefit from some ice breaking games and processes that help participants to greet one another and introduce themselves.

Name Games

Name Mirror - (10-50+ players, moderately active).

The group stands in a circle. The leader says, shouts, or sings, their name while making a movement. All the participants repeat the movement and say that person's name in the way they did. The next participant says their name and makes their own movement that is then copied by everyone and so on until everyone has told their name and made their movement.

Name Throw - (6-18 players, moderately active).

The players stand in a circle. The leader says his or her own name and throws a soft ball to a player across the circle. That person says his or her name and throws to someone else. This continues until all the players have told their names.

Variation 1 - (6-18 players, moderately active).
After this first round the leader says the name of a player and throws the soft ball to that person who names another player and throws the ball to them. This continues until all the players have been named.

Variation 2 – Rumpelstiltskin - (6-30 players, moderately active).
Useful for larger groups where there are a lot of names to remember. As with the first variation, except if a player does not remember the name of the person to whom they are going to throw the ball they call that player, 'Rumpelstiltskin.' That person replies, 'my name is not Rumpelstiltskin, it is…' The entire group says that players name, after which that person throws the ball to someone else saying that player's name.

Timbuktu - (6-12 players, low activity).

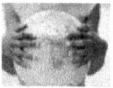

People greet one another with a handshake. The first person says, "How do you do, I'm from Timbuktu. My name is…'
The second person responds with,
'How do you do, I'm from Timbuktu, too. My name is…'
This continues until everyone has greeted everyone else.

Name Ripple - (6-18 players, moderately active). Good for re-enforcing names already heard.

The group stands in a circle. The leader says, shouts, or sings, the name of a person in the circle while making a movement. The person next to them and then on around the circle copies the way in which the leader has said the name and made the movement until it reaches that person. That person then gives another person's name and makes a movement that goes around the circle until it reaches the person named. This is repeated until everyone has been named.

Three Things – (12–50+ players, moderately active).

3

Three Things is an activity that gives people an opportunity to voice some of their thoughts on a topic while getting to know one another. This is a useful process because it introduces music, gets people moving, connects them to one another, gets people thinking and starts the listening process.
Participants form pairs in the centre of the room. They are instructed to each say three other things - their name and two other things about themselves such as where they come from and their favorite color.
When possible lively music is then played and the pairs break up and people move around the room in whatever way feels appropriate to the occasion – dancing to lively music for example.
After a short while, the music is paused and participants find another

person to pair up with. They are instructed to say their name and two other things about themselves. These could be such things as their favorite food, film or holiday destination and their reason for coming to the event. The music recommences and participants move again and so on until all or most people have spoken to one another and said a lot about themselves.

Suggested things to say are:
- ➢ Where you live.
- ➢ Which country, county or part of town you come from.
- ➢ Which organisation/stakeholder group you represent.
- ➢ Your interest in the topic of this meeting.
- ➢ Your major concern about this issue.
- ➢ Three words that would best describe how you feel about this topic.
- ➢ The change you would like to see take place in this situation.
- ➢ The outcome you most want from this event.

Favorite colors, food, comedians, films, TV programmes help keep the process light.

By the end of this process, attendees will have learned quite a lot about their fellow participants in a simple and fun way in a short time. In large gatherings, threes or even fours instead of pairs will take less time.

Postcard Snap - (10-30 players, low activity).

Obtain new or old, used postcards, photos or small pictures with clear images and cut each one in half, (one full card for every two participants). Shuffle the halves and place them face down in a dish or shallow basket. Invite participants to each take half a card and then move around the room introducing themselves to other participants, as they try to find the person with the other half.

When they have found that person, they learn what they can about each other to be able to introduce one another to the rest of the group. Such as, the person's name, where they are from, the work they are engaged in, and what they would like to achieve by the end of the meeting/event or anything else appropriate to the event.

Famous Name Game - (6-30 players, low activity).

The objectives of the famous Name Game are to break the ice by giving participants something interesting to do, whilst waiting for other participants to arrive. It also allows them a fun and comfortable way of meeting strangers. The added benefit is that it is a process in which they can start to hone their listening skills in preparation for the event that follows.

Preparation:

The leader writes the names of famous people clearly on sticky address labels, a different name for each label. Famous people can be from current times or from history, from the fields of politics, film, the arts, they can be authors or fictional characters. It is important that the names chosen are likely to be known to the players. Young people might not know film stars from previous eras and older folk may not be familiar with current rap performers. Enough labels need to be written for all the players with a few extra for quick guessers.

The game can start as soon as around six people have arrived and it ends when everyone has guessed their name or has turned up and had some time to attempt to do so - apart from extreme latecomers.

The leader informs the first few players and then others as they arrive that the object of the Game is to discover the name of the famous person written on a label that will be stuck to their backs.

These are the guidelines:

Players can ask only CLOSED questions such as:

'Is this person alive?'

'Is this person female?'

'Is this person a film star?'

Etc.

Players may ONLY respond to questions using the words:

'Yes.'

'No.'

'I don't know.'

(It might be helpful to have some info written up on a flip chart or whiteboard.)

FAMOUS NAME GAME

Players can ask only CLOSED questions such as:
'Is this person alive?'
'Is this person female?'
'Is this person a film star?'
Etc.

Players may ONLY respond to questions using the words:
'Yes.'
'No.'
'I don't know.'

HAVE FUN!

Each player introduces him or herself to someone and asks that person a closed question that could help them to guess their famous name. Once they have asked that person 1 question and answered that person's question they then move round the room and ask other people 1 question and answer their 1 question.

When they have asked and answered 1 question from each person they can then ask and answer 1 further question from anyone and so on until they guess their famous name. When this is accomplished the name is then stuck on the front of that person's clothing. They then help people who have not yet guessed their famous name.

If some people guess their name quickly another name can be stuck on their backs.

(It has been known for players to keep their labels visible and choose to be called that name for the duration of the event!)

Other icebreakers

There Ain't No Flies On Us - (8-50+ players, low activity).

Start with two lines of people, twenty feet apart facing each other. One line starts by taking a step toward the other and quietly and calmly saying:
"There ain't no flies on us.
There ain't no flies on us.
There may be flies on you guys,
But there ain't no flies on us."
The other line then takes a step forward and also says the same words to the first line. The lines keep doing this until they are directly in front of each other, all the time getting louder. When they get within arms-reach of one another, suggest a handshake or hug and exchange of names with a few of the people, to show no hard feelings.

When this is played at the beginning of an event it can be played again at the end with a slight change in wording to emphasis the connection made during the event.
Change of wording:
"There ain't no flies on you.
There ain't no flies on you.
There ain't no flies on us guys,
And there ain't no flies on you."

Partnering Games

As well as the usual request for people to, 'Partner with a person you do/do not know well,' it can be useful to have some fun ways to randomly partner people up or group them together.

Same, same - (6-50 players+, low activity).

Leader says, 'Partner up with one other person who…'

Suggested pairings could be: is also wearing something in a color you are wearing, a similar type of shoe, has similar to your hair color, is wearing spectacles, is also not wearing spectacles, etc.

See also Postcard Snap

Getting into groups - (6–50+ players, low activity).

Decide how many people you want in each group and divide the number of people present by that number. Have everyone stand in a circle. If, for example you want groups of six people, have the first person identify themselves as number one the next as number two and so on until number six is identified. The next person in the circle counts themselves as one, the next as two and so on until everyone has a number. All the people with the same number form a group, which in this case would be groups of six people.

Fingers - (6-50 players, low activity).

People are asked, at a given signal, to raise one, two, three fingers. People get together in the desired numbers with others who have the same number of fingers raised (e.g., get together in groups of four with people who have the same number of fingers raised as you do).

Energizing Games

The following games could be useful for re-energizing people who are flagging after a period of concentration or in the post lunch energy dip, to round off a session or before starting one. Some of these games can also be icebreakers.

Energy - (5-50+ players, low activity).

The group stands in a circle, holding hands. The leader through a hand squeeze passes the "energy" around the circle in an anti-clockwise direction from his or her right hand to the left hand of the person on his or her right. After the energy has been passed around and through everyone at least once, the leader can reverse the flow by sending the energy back the way it came with two hand squeezes in the opposite direction – from their left hand to the right hand of the person on their left.

Then the direction of the flow of energy can be changed by anyone at any time with one squeeze from his or her right hand or two squeezes from their left. This often leads to energy running around the group in several directions at once and changing direction quickly. A variation is to play this game with eyes closed.

Rainstorm - (5–50+ players, low activity).

Players stand or sit in a circle. The leader makes the first sound and movement, which is a gentle breathing sound and flowing arm movements indicating a gentle breeze. Everyone copies the sound and movement. The leader then makes a louder whooshing noise to show the wind getting stronger. The leader gauges when to introduce each consecutive sound to build into a rainstorm. Sounds could include: shushing, rubbing hands together, finger snapping, tongue clucking, thigh slapping, chest thumping, hand clapping, foot stamping and shouting.

Variation

After the loudest noise has reached a crescendo the leader indicates the lessening of the storm by reversing the noises all the way back to the gentle breathing sound. At the end the group holds hands and stands perfectly still for a few moments in the peace following the storm.

A-Rum-Sum-Sum - (5-50+ players, low activity).

Seated in a circle, "A Rum Sum Sum", is sung by everyone while alternately patting hands to knees, the "Goodie's" are sung with alternating hand pats to the chest and the "A Rah Man' is sung while extending arms over the head and bowing into the circle. The words of the song are:

First verse:
A rum sum sum, a rum sum sum.
Goodie, goodie, goodie, goodie, goodie.
Rum sum sum. (repeat)
Second verse:
A rah man, a rah man.
Goodie, goodie, goodie, goodie, goodie.
Rum sum sum. (repeat)

Fire Engine - (10-50+ players, active)

Lines of about 5 people are fire engines in a Firehouse at one end of the room from where there will be a fire. The leader rings a bell or makes some nose to indicate the fire alarm. The first fire engine in each line goes to put out the fire. However, it's a big fire, and the engine must go back to her/his line to get another engine, repeating this until all the engines in their line have been brought to put out the fire. This often becomes competitive as each Firehouse races to be the first to get all their engines to the fire.

Fruit Basket - (10-30 players, active).

In a seated circle with just enough chairs, everyone tells their favorite fruit. The leader (the shopper) stands in the middle and says which fruits she or he needs for her or his fruit basket – orange, apple, mango etc. When several have been named she/he says, "Go", which is the signal for all those who named those fruits to go to a new chair, including the leader. Whoever is left is the new shopper. After a while, someone can call "Fruit Basket" when everyone changes chairs - not one next to them.

Detective - (5-50+ players, moderate activity).

The group stands in a circle. One or more people are chosen as the detective. Their task: find the leader of the "gang." One person starts the game as the leader by making a movement that the group quickly copies to hide the identity of that leader. The detective(s) attempt to identify that leader. Whether or not they successfully do so another person makes another movement that the group again quickly copies to hide the identity of that leader. The detective(s) attempts to identify each person who changes the movement. The leader needs to change at least every 10 seconds. The role of detective also needs to change regularly.

Elephant, Rabbit, Palm Tree - (10-50 players, moderate activity).

The leader, standing in the middle of the circle, points at someone and says the person's name and says "rabbit", or "palm tree", or "elephant." The person pointed at makes teeth, branches, or a trunk, as appropriate, with their hand(s). The people on either side of this person then copy that person by making the same movement for ears/branches/trunk for the animal or plant mentioned and so on around the circle. When everyone has copied the movement someone new goes into the middle. Not everyone in a large group will need to name the animal/plant.

La-Ba-Doo - (10-50+ players, moderate activity).

Form a close circle with arms on shoulders. The dance step is a simple side step, step together, and the tune is the same as "Merrily we roll along". The words are:

"Now we do the La-Ba-Doo,
La-Ba-Doo, La-Ba-Doo,
Now we do the La-Ba-Doo,
La-Ba-Doo, La-Ba-Doo, Hey!"

The "hey" is accompanied by a vigorous foot stomp. Then the song is immediately repeated going in the opposite direction. Then the La-Ba-Doo dance is done with hands on head (and then with fingers in ears, then on nose, hands on stomach, on knees and finally fingers on toes) changing direction with each, Hey!

Tiny Tim - (6-50+ players, active).

Lines with five or so people are formed. The first person in each line is Tiny Tim, the other people behind him are members of his family: mother, father, little sister, big brother, grandparents, Spot the Dog, Tom the cat, etc. Have the players identify which role they play. The leader acts as storyteller. Every time one of the family members or pets is mentioned in the story, the person playing that role must run around their group by going down to the front, up round the back and return to their original place in the line. If "all" are mentioned, they all go.

Look Up - (10-35 players, low activity).

There are 2 circles of players. One person is chosen in each circle to be the caller. Everyone looks down at his or her feet. The caller for each circle says "Look up!" and everyone looks up at someone in their circle. If two people are looking at each other, they both go into the other circle. If the caller is looking at someone who is looking at him or her they both leave the circle and a new caller is chosen.

My Aunt Comes From... - (5-50+ players, moderate activity).

Leader starts by saying to group, "My aunt (uncle, cousin, any relation) comes from New York (or any other place you can think of) and she/he walks like this." The leader proceeds to demonstrate an exaggerated "walk" that the whole group copies for at least 5 seconds. From then on anyone can clap and show a new "walk" of one of their "relatives" from wherever.

Frogs into Princes – (6-50+ players, active).

In pairs, one person is a frog and the other person is a large fish trying to catch and eat the frog. After 5 to 10 seconds the leader says that the frog in each pair turns into an otter that tries to catch the fish. After another few seconds the fish turns into a bear trying to catch the otter. Then the otter turns into a prince trying to catch the bear. The bear then turns into a witch who chases the prince and by touch turns him into a frog.

All change - (10-30 players, active).

Everyone is in a circle of chairs. One person stands in the middle and calls out an instruction for people to move to other chairs, something like 'everyone who is wearing something white is to move to another chair.' While they are moving the person in the middle – who in this instance must be wearing something white - sits on a chair and whoever is left without a seat is a new caller. That caller then calls out something else to make people change seats. If the caller wants to be replaced they have to call out something that applies to them. At any time the caller can shout 'All change!' and everyone has to move to another seat – not the one next to them.

Shoe stomp - (10-50 players, active).

The group kneels in a circle, with everyone holding one of their shoes in each of their hands. The leader passes the stomp around the circle in an anti-clockwise direction by hitting the floor with the shoe in his or her right hand. The person on their right copies this movement and so on around the circle. After the stomp has gone around the circle at least once, the leader can send the stomp in the opposite direction by hitting the floor twice with the shoe in their left hand which is copied by the person on their left.

Then the direction of the stomping can be changed by anyone at any time with one stomp with the shoe in their right hand or with two stomps with the shoe in their left. This leads to the stomp running around the group in several directions at once and changing direction quickly.

Tag games

In some situations the tagging can be done with small, soft cushions – not to be thrown at people.

Everybody's 'It' - (5-50+ players, active).

Everybody is "it" and can tag everyone else. Once you are tagged however, you freeze until the end of the game (which comes quickly). If someone runs too near a frozen person, the frozen person can unfreeze an arm to reach out and freeze the runner.

Partner Tag - (10-50+ players, active).

Participants are paired randomly. This is a tag game between the 2 people in each pair. Everyone in the group walks around trying to tag their partner while being careful to avoid collisions with other participants. If a collision occurs, they shake hands with the person who they bumped into and say, "I'm very sorry, it won't happen again." The next stage is to walk more quickly and then to jog. Running could be the final option if all the participants are able to do so.

Hug tag - (10-40 players, active).

There is one 'it' who carries a cushion to tag people with. When tagged that person becomes 'it'. A person is safe from being tagged while another person is hugging them. This hug can only last for a few seconds and then when the leader shouts 'move' each person must move again. After the game has been going for a few minutes another 'it' is added. If it is a large group a further 'it' can be added a little later.

Base Tag - (10-30 players, active).

TAG!

This is a tag game with several "its," about one for every 5 players. The 'its' try to tag the non-its, thereby transferring their "it-ness." No one tags back. There are a number of bases, about one for every three players. When a 'non-it' steps on a base, he/she cannot be tagged. However, if another non-it comes to the base and says "G0!" the person on the base must leave immediately.

Cats and Mice - (10-50 players, active).

A Cat is in the middle of a square or rectangular 'field'. All the "Mice" are on one side of the 'field' along a boundary. When the Cat says "Go" the Mice must cross the field to the other side, where they are safe again. The

Cat tags Mice, turning them into Mousetraps. Mousetraps can move and try to catch Mice to hold on to them until the Cat can tag them. Mousetraps have to call for the Cat to come by shouting, "Cat, cat, cat!" Continue until all are caught, or just one is left.

Three's A Crowd - (10-30 players, active).

There is an "it" and a "non-it". The other players are arranged around the room standing in pairs, one in front of the other. The "It" tries to catch and tag the "non-it". If successful, the roles reverse. Either player can go to the front of any pair of players, immediately turning the player in the back of that pair into the role of the person. It can help if the "it" says, "You're it!" to help the back person know they are the chaser.

Wizards - (10–50+ players, active).

There are to be about 1 Wizard to every five other players. The Wizards try to freeze non-Wizards by running their hand down the back of a person. Frozen people can be un-frozen with a hug from another person who is not frozen.

Quick Energizers - (10–50+ players, variously active).

    a.   Everyone stands up and stretchers.
    b.   Everyone stands up and does star jumps.
    c.   Everyone is asked to change places with someone at the opposite side of the circle or table.
    d.   A ball or small beanbag is thrown around the group or two or three balls can be thrown around at the same time if the group is a large one.
    e.   Each person taps his or her breastbone rapidly.
    f.   Each person does chest thumping and Gorilla type movements

accompanied by appropriate noises.

g. Everyone rubs their stomach and taps their head at the same time then changing to doing one first and then the other and then doing it in reverse.

Cooperative Games

Knots - (6-12 players in each group, moderate activity).

Players stand in a circle close together putting their hands in a clump in the middle and mingling them. Everyone then closes their eyes and takes a hand in each of theirs. Upon opening eyes, check to see that everyone holds a hand of two different players. Players then, without losing contact, try to untangle into a circle. To add challenge, see that players do not take the hand of the person next to them.

Three-Legged Soccer - (12-30 players, active).

Pairs of players are tied together at the ankle, making mobility interesting and reducing the competition level. Also, it's best to use a "ball" that doesn't roll to fast or far. Maybe even a cushion will do.
Variations
    If the group is a large one teams can be selected.
    And/or
    Have two pairs play goalkeeper, one at either end of the 'field'.

Squaring the circle - (20-50+ players, moderate activity).

All players stand in a circle with eyes closed. Using their intuition and keeping their eyes closed they attempt to turn the circle into a square. The leader monitors progress and calls out 'stop' when the task is accomplished or time is up.

Lap Sit – (12-50+ players, low activity).

This is also a trust building game. Everyone, including the leader stands very close together touching front to back all facing the same way in a circle. The leader explains that on a count of '123 sit!' everyone is going to sit carefully down on the lap of the person behind them and that it is vital for everyone to sit down at the same time. After the excitement and trepidation has died down the leader does the count. As soon as everyone is sitting get the group to immediately stand up again. Now do it again and this time they stay sitting for a second or two. If this has worked well, do it once more and when the group is sitting once again they are instructed to slowly and gently walk forward together, still sitting, on the command of, '1,2,3, right foot - left foot – and so on.' After a few steps the group might start to wobble so they are asked to gently stand up together.

When this game is played successfully, the players achieve a great sense of accomplishment. This is very bonding! I have seen this successfully completed by groups of over 100 people.

Trust building games

Trust Walk - (6-50+ players, moderate activity).

In pairs the participants decide who will be a 'blind' person being led first and who will be the sighted guide. The 'blind' person chooses to be blindfolded or trusts him or herself to keep their eyes closed. The pair links arms and move slowly around the room with the guide carefully steering the 'blind' person away from obstacles and other people. Speed can increase as trust has developed between them. After a few minutes they change roles.
Variation
The 'blind' person keeps contact with their guide by the slightest of touch on their arm.

The Blind Leading The Blind - (6-30 players, moderate activity).

The players get into groups of threes. Two players are going to be 'blind' and the remaining person will be a guide dog. The 'blind' players can choose to be blindfolded or not. They hold onto one another by linking arms, each of them leaving an arm free. They begin to move slowly around the room with the guide dog walking in front of them calling out instructions for avoiding people and other obstacles. The 'blind' people can also assist their progress by feeling their way around the room. After a while they may feel safe to speed up and only slow down again if the dog gives a warning. Everyone has a turn in the blindfolded roles.

Trust teams - (8-40 players, moderate activity).

The players get into groups of fours. One player is going to be 'blind' and the remaining people will be guide dogs. For this the 'blind' players are to be blindfolded. One guide dog walks in front of the 'blind' person and the other two walk very closely on either side, although not holding the person. The group moves around the room with the guide dog giving stop, go or slow down commands and the two side guides nudging the 'blind' player to go left or right of obstacles or other people. Speed can increase with the level of trust. Everyone has a turn in the blindfolded role.

This may take some time and can be a good game for building trust in small groups or teams.

Touch and tell - (6-40 players, moderate activity).

In pairs the participants decide who will lead and who will be led first. The person being led chooses to be blindfolded or trust him or herself to keep their eyes closed. The person leading holds the underneath of the forearm of the person being led, leaving that person's hand free to feel the things they are guided to touch. This would be best to be their right hand if that person is right-handed or left if they are left hand.

The guide leads their 'blind' person around the room gently placing that persons feeling hand on areas or items of differing textures and shapes. These can be the furniture and furnishings, plants, vases of flowers, bowls of water, sculptures, pieces of wood, stones or pebbles etc. This can be done in silence or it could have been decided by the group beforehand that the person being led will say what it is they think they are feeling. After a while they change roles.

Cars - (6-40 players, moderate activity).

In pairs, participants decide who will be the car and who will be the driver. The driver stands behind the car with his or her hands gently holding the tops of the person's arms at shoulder level. The person in the car role closes his or her eyes. (Blindfolds can be worn, however the object of the game is for participants to trust themselves as well as trusting each other).

Each driver starts their engine and moves the car around the room. The driver stops, starts and steers the car with the appropriate pressure on the tops of the 'cars' arms. They drive slowly at first and then gradually gathering speed as trust is developed between car and driver. Care must be taken to avoid collision with any other cars or any obstacles. The car can request to slow down or halt at any time they feel uncomfortable or unsafe. The car and driver change roles.

In all these games people can choose to be blindfolded or to be trusted and to trust themselves to keep their eyes closed.

These games can also be played outside if the conditions are safe enough.

Robots - (6-36 players, moderate activity).

Form groups of three, one is a robot master for the other two "robots". The threesome decide upon their warning phrase or noise for when the robots meet an obstacle, a boundary or another robot. The robot masters start their robots who walk off in different directions stiffly and in a straight line. The robot master has to keep an eye on both robots at the same time. When a robot meets an obstacle, they sound their alarm noise or phrase, and the master must come to turn them away from the obstacle. Switch roles so that everyone can be a robot master. If numbers aren't perfect, there can be one or two groups of 4.

Trust Fall - (6-60 players, moderate activity).

This game is only to be played if there are enough people in each group to safely catch anyone falling.

Participants get into groups of around six to ten people. There needs to be at least one person strong enough to guarantee that any person falling will be safely caught.

The person to fall first in each group folds their arms closely across their chest. He or she stands with their back to the group who are lined up in pairs in the appropriate position ready to catch them.

When everyone is ready the person falls backwards and is caught by the group and lowered gently and then stood up on their feet again. Then the next person gets ready to fall.

Connecting Games

The development of trust can be enhanced when people feel physically comfortable with one another. The following games are helpful in achieving this by providing appropriate opportunities for people to touch or to hold onto one another.

Huddle Up - (8-50+ players, low activity).

The group is asked to mingle about in and around one another until the leader says loudly "Huddle up", plus a command, such as: "Huddle up with people wearing the same color shirt." In this case all those with the same color tops then quickly get together in a huddle. After a few calls the leader can invite other people to make the call. Examples of calls are: color or type of any clothing – jeans, shorts, skirts, etc. or of shoes, color or length of hair, wearing spectacles, earrings, watches, belts, anything that is obvious. The last instruction is, 'Huddle up with everyone'.

Car wash - (6-50+ players, low activity).

The players stand in two lines facing one another at a distance far enough apart for people to walk between. A person from one end of the line walks through the 'carwash' to the other end while being sprayed, washed, rinsed and polished in succession as they progress through the 'car wash'. The carwash functions are divided between the people consecutively down the line with the first few people offering the spraying service.

The spraying and the rinsing are done with light finger tapping on the 'car' body or sprinkling movements around it. The washing is done through massaging movements and the polishing is done with smoothing strokes down the body or around it. All body touching is done appropriately and respectfully.

Each person in the role of the 'car' states his or her preference for a light, medium or heavy wash. When that 'car' has gone through the 'car wash' they park at that end of the line and become part of the 'car wash' and join in the polishing.

The person who stood opposite them at the beginning of the line now becomes the 'car' and so on. As each part of the 'carwash' become 'cars' their role in the car wash is taken over by the next person down the line and so on so that eventually everybody in the 'car wash' plays each part of the car washing process.

If the group is more than twenty-four then each 'car' enters the car wash when the 'car' in front of them has gone through the spraying process. If the group is even larger there can be two 'car washes'. The game ends when every 'car' has been 'washed'.

Rain shower - (10–50+ players, low activity).

This is similar although more gentle than the previous game. The group forms two lines and one person walks down the middle and is showered with gentle rain from the participants they pass. In a small group the next person starts to walk through the shower when the first person has reached the end. In a larger group the second person starts to walk through the shower when the first person has past half a dozen people.

People to People - (8–40 players, moderate activity).

People are in pairs in a circle with the leader in the middle. The leader calls out two body parts, which the partners must put together on each other, such as Finger to nose' or right elbow to left knee'. After two or three calls, leader calls "people to people", at which point all partners separate and move to get a new partner, including the leader. The person left without a partner becomes the new leader.

Quack! - (8-50 players, moderately active).

Everyone moves backwards, walking slightly bent over, hands on knees. If a person bumps another, they line up, bum-to-bum, look down between their legs so that they see the other person, and greet the other with a "Quack!"

Gentle Connecting Games

Ironing Board - (6–50+ players, low activity).

In pairs each person of the pair take turns "ironing" the other person's clothes while that person is wearing them (in appropriate areas, obviously).

Shop window mannequin – (6-40 players, low activity).

In pairs, one person is a mannequin in a shop window who is dressed from head to toe by a shop assistant who positions the mannequin in poses to attract the attention of passing shoppers. Change roles.

Sculptures – (6-40 players, low activity).

In pairs one person becomes the sculptor and one is the clay that is going to be sculpted. The sculptor gently, slowly and respectfully moves, prods, pushes the clay into the sculpted shape he or she wishes to create. The clay allows themselves to be shaped and to hold the position that the sculptor places them in. The sculptor needs to be careful to not place their sculpture in a pose that would be difficult to maintain.

This takes around a minute and when it is completed all the sculptors move around and admire one another's artistic creations. Then the artist and the clay swap places.

Mirror Mirror – (6-40 players, low activity).

In pairs, one person makes slow movements in front of the 'mirror'; the other person must copy their movements. Change roles after a while. After this both people can make movements and use their intuition to keep in sync with one another.

Spaghetti Sauce – (6-50+ players, low activity).

In pairs, one person is spaghetti taking whatever shape they imagine spaghetti to take. The other person is spaghetti sauce trying to cover as much of the spaghetti is possible. Change roles.

Gentle rain – (6-50+ players, low activity).

In pairs one person is a shower of rain tapping their partner from head to toe down their back with raindrops. Change roles.

These two are quick games for when there seems a need for closer connections and time is short.

Games with messages

Chinese Whispers - (6-40 players, low activity).

Large groups can be divided into smaller groups of around 8 people.

A short message is whispered in the ear of the first person in the group who whispers it to the next and so on until everyone in the group has received the whispered message.

Although the message ought not to be too complex it might be interesting for it to contain some directions and a date or numbers.

The last person in each group to receive the message then says it out loud for all to hear. The person who first delivered the message then says out loud the original message.

Note the changes to the message that have been made along the way. If more than one group plays at the same time use the same message and compare the results!

Chinese Movements - (6-18 players, low activity).

Circle game, players stand or sit facing out. One player stands in middle. Then taps someone on the back. That 2nd player turns around. Player in center makes a simple movement and returns to circle, facing in. 2nd player goes in middle then taps a 3rd player & repeats the movement then returns to circle, facing in. This goes on till last player is shown movement and everyone else is facing in. Last player & first meet in middle and at count of three do movement.

Note any changes that may have been made to the movement during the process. Both these games are examples of how things can become altered through individual interpretation.

Equal Distance – (6-50+ players, low to moderate activity).

The chairs are moved to the edges of the room. The participants stand and identify two other people in the room, without letting those people or anyone else know which people they have chosen.

Each person then moves to a place in the room that is at equal distance between those two people. This may take a while because as everyone moves about, the distances between people will keep changing. Towards the end of the game, the movements are likely to become quite small adjustments to people's positions.

Occasionally, even at a late stage, someone may decide to move to an entirely different part of the room in order to achieve their goal. This is likely to create some chaos and laughter.

When everyone is finally standing still it might be appropriate to point out that in this game, as in life, every action we take is likely to have an effect upon the people around us.

Useful extras

The signal for silence

This is useful to save time and protect the voices of leaders and callers. A leader or anyone who needs to be listened to when giving instructions or directions stands still and silent with their right arm raised. Anyone seeing this copies them by standing still and silent with their own arm raised. Everyone stands in that position until the whole group is silently paying attention.

This signal can be used effectively at any time when silence is required during a meeting or event.

Connecting to the ground

Indoors, whenever circumstances and furnishings allow, encourage participants to play in bare feet. Socks can be worn on carpeted areas if preferred, although be aware of actions that may move onto uncarpeted areas upon which socks might slip.

Rock Paper Scissors

This can be played at any time in pairs or threes when deciding which person is to go first in a process. Scissors cut paper, paper wraps rock, rock breaks scissors. The person who wins is the person to go first.

Appreciation

At the end of a game, especially those played in pairs or small groups, players could be encouraged to show their appreciation of one another in whatever way they feel appropriate.

Feedback

Particularly in trust building in connecting games it can be supportive to provide opportunity for the players who have been together to share with one another what the experience gave them. This could include how safe or otherwise they felt with the other person, and/or any emotion that arose for them during the game.

Games can break down social and structural divides and can quickly connect people with one another. Because for some people, games revive unhappy memories of embarrassment or failure, strongly emphasize that all these games are cooperative and have no winners or losers. Games are supposed to be fun!

These are some examples of group games that I have collected over the years. Research in books shops and on line could provide you with more. Enjoy!

4

APPLYING PROCESSES TO TRICKY
SITUATIONS

Participants and meeting managers will both experience tricky situations during meetings from time to time. Some situations result from poorly managed meetings, which we have already addressed. Others can result from unfortunate attitudes, poor communication skills and inappropriate behavior of some participants. Many of the most common of these attitudes and behaviors are described in this section, as are some suggested options for dealing with them.

Whilst many of these options will require action from meeting managers, participants familiar with some of the suggested processes could assist in handling them. The following suggestions are made to help in dealing with situations that might derail meetings, detrimentally affect the outcomes or undermine group cohesion.

The following suggested options could be especially useful in chaired meetings where the rigid structure and constraints of formal meetings can lead participants to feel restrained or controlled. This may result in conflict between participants or expressions of frustration or their use of covert methods of manipulation. It may also lead to challenges to the meeting manager.

The need for them ought to be less likely in facilitated meetings. This is because the procedures and processes usually used in facilitation are specifically designed to promote cooperative engagement and respectful interaction.

Persistent latecomers

Occasional lateness might be unavoidable. However, some people are persistently late for almost everything. This might be because they are inefficient with the use of their time, they may try to do too many things in the time available, or they have little respect for other people's time. Whatever the reason for their behavior, none of these are valid reasons for delaying the start of a meeting.

When they eventually arrive, unless the latecomers are significant presenters of information, it could be sensible to avoid spending a lot of time introducing them or bringing them up to speed as this can prolong the meeting and frustrate the people who are already engaged. It might also support the latecomer's attitudes to timekeeping or play into any need they might have for getting attention.

It is the responsibility of the latecomers to make their entrance discretely and to engage in the meeting with as little disruption to proceedings as possible.

Options:

➢ Smile, welcome them and continue with the meeting.

➢ Have a quiet word afterwards about their persistent lateness.

Everyone talking at once

There are some situations when discussions become heated or everyone wants to talk and no one wants to listen.

Options:

➢ Move from content to process. By 'calling attention' to what is going on the awareness is drawn away from the content of what is being said and towards the process of communication. For example, you might say one of the following: 'I am finding it difficult to follow these arguments when so many people are talking at the same time.' 'I know there are people wanting to offer good ideas and share their experience and I would like to be able to hear them clearly and without disruption.' This approach indicates to all those present that the style of the exchange is unhelpful without attacking anyone's ideas or position.

➢ A Go-Round would be appropriate at this time so that everyone has a chance to address the subject.

➢ No one speaks twice… would also be a helpful process.

Reticent contributors

New members, shy people, or timid communicators may feel reticent about offering their opinions, so these people are sometimes overlooked or marginalized when their wisdom and experience could be beneficial to the meeting.

Options:

- ➢ Go-Rounds can help them to gain confidence in speaking up in meetings.
- ➢ Occasionally encourage them to say something on the subject under discussion.
- ➢ They may feel less exposed or put on the spot if they are asked for their contribution after others have made theirs.
- ➢ Ease them into contributing by seeking their opinion on non-contentious issues or by asking them easy questions.
- ➢ Increase their self-confidence by gently pointing out that their views are important and their contribution is valuable.
- ➢ Give credit whenever possible.

Hostility and aggression

Hostile and aggressive people might want their own way or may intend to get the better of other individuals in the group. They might run down or demean people by being critical and judgmental. For them, winning a point or succeeding in arguments could be more important than a successful outcome to the meeting.

Options:

- ➢ Require the use of 'I' statements.
- ➢ Ask 'How does this help?'
- ➢ Constructively listen to bring out the person's underlying reasons for their behavior.
- ➢ Set up a short 'I heard you say' session between the hostile person and the one to whom they are being hostile.
- ➢ Ask for a reality check from the group to indicate the level of agreement about any criticism.
- ➢ Take a Moment.
- ➢ Call attention to the hostility.

Addressing the hostility directly brings it into the open for processing. 'Stan, you seem to be very critical of this suggestion. Is there a reason for what appears to be hostile behavior?' This can direct Stan's aggression away from the person making the suggestion and focus on Stan's concerns. It might however, re-direct the hostility toward you as the manager of the meeting.

It is useful to remember that in most groups there is often a little hostility towards the leader, just because he or she has assumed or been given some power and authority. Whether or not you are the leader of the group, in managing the meeting you may be perceived as taking a leadership role. By recognizing and accept this, you can further the purpose of the meeting by absorbing some amount of the hostility.

Effective group leaders may be willing to occasionally be a bit of a scapegoat. This relieves pressure and lets the group get on with business. Hostility has to go somewhere, and if the leader doesn't take it, the group cohesion might be weakened.

For example a leader could say something like 'Stan, I can see that you are against Mary's suggestion of the school hall. I understand that you are annoyed that we can't have use of the Town Hall for the event. I want you to know that I take responsibility for that. Perhaps I could have been more persistent in asking for it than I was. I am sorry.' This approach can lessen hostility and aggression from people who look to find fault. By taking responsibility, a leader can save time in meetings by removing the need for some people to search for someone to blame.

If a group member is persistently hostile, the meeting manager could have a quiet word with him or her or delegate this task to someone in the group who has the appropriate communication skills.

Regular hostile exchanges

When these regularly occur between the same two people this might indicate that there is history between them. In this case you could request that these two sort out their differences outside of meeting times. Someone with experience could mediate this interaction.

If people are unwilling to manage their behavior and hostility continues to detrimentally affect meetings, it might be beneficial to ask the group for a reality check on their attitudes to these people. In extreme cases and after every effort has been made to resolve the hostility the consensus of the group might require one or both of these people to leave.

Dealing with pessimists, rejecters and defeatists

Pessimists and defeatists may feel that problems are insurmountable and see no point in trying to solve them. They may be lacking in confidence, have low self-belief or because they might expect to fail they give up easily. Some pessimists and defeatists might become rejecters and by finding fault with all suggested solutions or tediously nitpicking every detail, they might, consciously or unconsciously, undermine or sabotage progress.

Options:
  ➤ Ask people to reframe their objections into positive solutions.

➤ Ask them for one positive suggestion that could improve the matter under discussion.
➤ Ask 'How does this help?'
➤ Calling attention and constructively listening might expose their attitudes and genuine reasons for their pessimism.
➤ Have a quiet word afterwards.
➤ Treat defeatism as a legitimate opinion. Whenever a defeatist makes a 'that won't work' statement, reply with something like, 'Thank you Fred. We will note that your opinion is that this will not work and that we should not try it.' Then move on. By treating defeatism as a consistent 'no' vote it releases others in the meeting to get on with making positive contributions.

Grenade throwers

These people often wait for an opportune moment that is likely to have a significantly negative effect on the meeting in which to express an opinion, make a point, or reveal some information. Their intention may be to create disruption, undermine the proceedings or just gain some attention for themselves. When these 'grenades' are thrown right at the last minute they could be intending to sabotage decisions.

Although these people are often considered to be annoying or arrogant, in my experience their actions are often based on insecurity or the expectation that they will not be taken seriously or listened to respectfully.

Options:
➤ Ask them for a solution to the problem that they have just stated.
➤ Ask 'How does this help?'
➤ Call attention.
➤ Do a reality check.
➤ Have a quiet word afterwards.

On the other hand

These people may not be intending to be difficult. They might be those types of people who 'sort by difference'. That means that they see those things that stand out from the norm, those things that are different from the expected. They see the bits that are missing or when things are not what they seem to be.

What they have to say might be unpopular. They may be considered to be harbingers of doom or negative thinkers because they are pointing out the pitfalls in arguments and reasons why suggestions might not work. Their experience could be useful and their information may very well be correct, however, it might not be what the rest of the meeting wants to hear.

Their constant pointing out of glitches in arguments and faults in thinking may have alienated them in past meetings. Whenever they have tried to bring attention to their concerns they may have been shouted down and rudely treated or ignored. People who sought by difference often find themselves to be marginalized in meetings where positive thinking is desired or is the expected norm.

These people might in fact be very useful to have around. They often see things that others don't see. They're the ones who notice the missing details while everyone else is admiring the big picture.

It takes courage to suggest something that is going to be unpopular, time-consuming or costly. This type of person probably pointed out that there were not enough lifeboats on the Titanic!

Options:

➢ Call attention to discover what concerns this 'grenade' is really about.
➢ Ask 'How does this help?'
➢ Delay any decision so that this person can prepare a proper presentation about their concerns.
➢ If you are aware of this person's abilities before the meeting acknowledge their skill to them. If possible give him or her the task of identifying the glitches that could potentially cause problems. These could be presented to the meeting in order to be taken into account well before the time for decision-making.

Attention seekers

These are people who need to be noticed. They often interrupt with unnecessary remarks or questions. They might try to hog the limelight or become irritated if they think they are being ignored or that others are getting more attention than they are.

Options:

➢ Give these people tasks that will put them in the spotlight and yet keep them busy or quiet. Writing suggestions on a flipchart, leading a sub group, reporting back from a working group.
➢ Insisting on Parliamentary procedure might help where people have to be recognized by the chairperson before they can speak.
➢ Use the 'No one speaks twice… guideline and the two-minute rule.
➢ Employ strict timekeeping.
➢ Balance efficiency with compassion.

Narrators

These people might also have attention needs. They are likely to have stories to tell and examples to offer on almost any subject being discussed. They may go into lengthy, detailed explanations and might be skilled in bringing their own personal problems and experiences into almost any dialogue. They can blur the focus of discussions and take up a lot of meeting time.

Options:

- ➢ Remind these people of the time limitation of the meeting, bring them back to the point, and then if they continue, end their contribution on the matter in hand, 'thank you for your contribution' and move on.
- ➢ Invoke the two-minute rule.
- ➢ Ask 'How does this help?'
- ➢ Interrupt their stories to ask them what they intend to contribute to further the purpose of the meeting. If they have no useful contribution to make, cut their story short, 'thank you for your contribution' and move on.
- ➢ Balance efficiency with compassion.

Entertainers

These people are often funny and may appear to not take anything too seriously. This might be to cover their feelings of insecurity or their behavior may yet be another form of attention seeking. Although these people can help to keep a meeting light-hearted any inappropriate foolery can demean the proceedings.

Flippancy and sarcasm might be acceptable forms of humor to some people. However, these could be an indication of lack of respect for some people at the meeting or be a demonstration of having little interest in the matter under discussion.

Options:

- ➢ Thank these people for lightening the mood of the meeting and ask them for a positive contribution to the proceedings.
- ➢ Call attention by asking something like: 'I have heard you make several seemingly sarcastic remarks about these suggestions and I wonder if you have real concerns about them. Please tell us what they are?'
- ➢ Ask for all contributions to be made in 'I' statements.

Compulsive talkers

These people may have the need to keep their presence felt.

Options:
> - Maintain strict time-keeping.
> - Invoke the no one speaks twice… guideline.
> - Invoke the two-minute rule.

People with attitudes of superiority

People with these attitudes can intimidate or inhibit some people. They might undermine equality and may put a stop to the notion that discussions will be taking place among peers.

Options:
> - Require the use of inclusive language and remind everyone that they are in a peer group.
> - The two-minute rule and no one speaks twice can help in creating equal opportunities.
> - Have a quiet word afterwards.

Uncooperative people

Some people find it difficult to be cooperative and may never reach the cooperative stage in a group's development. While remaining extremely assertive these people can prolong meetings unnecessarily and prevent or undermine decision-making.

> The three stages of group development are described in detail in the book: SUCCESSFUL GROUPS & PROJECTS, in the YOU MAKE THE DIFFERENCE series.

Options:
> - Ask 'How does this help?'
> - Constructively listen to bring out any genuine concerns.
> - Call attention to the person's unwillingness to cooperate.
> - Ask for a reality check on their attitude.
> - Note their attitude and move on.
> - Have a quiet word afterwards.

People who like to dominate and control

These people might be so used to being in charge that they do not know how to not be. Some of these people may have held positions of power and responsibility. Often they know how to get things done and become frustrated and impatient with people they consider to be inefficient or incompetent. They may believe that their talents and experience are not being recognized. They might resent not being the leader of the group or managing the meeting and attempt, consciously or unconsciously, to undermine the meeting manager's role.

There might be a temptation to exclude such domineering or controlling people from the group. However, my experience is that these characteristics can be of great benefit to projects if used appropriately.

Options:

- ➤ Delegate some of your meeting management roles to these people.
- ➤ Put them in charge of important tasks where leadership and efficiency are required.
- ➤ If their frustration boils over in meetings, ask: 'How does this help?
- ➤ Engage them in Constructive Communication to bring their concerns into the open.
- ➤ Openly appreciate their skills and experience.
- ➤ Curtail their domination of discussions by invoking the no one speaks twice… guideline or the two-minute rule.
- ➤ Have a quiet word afterwards.

Persistent questioners

The asking of concise and succinct questions is a vital component of meetings. However, irrelevant or pointless questions can disrupt the flow and waste time on inconsequential matters. Persistent questioners might be trying to get attention or gain some control of the proceedings. They may be consciously or unconsciously attempting to undermine the role of the meeting manager.

Options:

- ➤ Employ strict time-keeping.
- ➤ Invoke the no one speaks twice…guideline.
- ➤ Ask: 'How does this help?'
- ➤ Ask for a reality check about the relevance of the questions.

Axe Grinders

These people may try to relate everything back to their pet thing, whether or not it has anything to do with the matter under discussion or the purpose of the meeting. They might have a fixation or an obsession about an issue, which could muddy the waters and waste time. Sometimes people misuse question time at the end of a meeting or a presentation as an opportunity to air their views and grind their axes, particularly if they have not had a chance to do so earlier in the meeting.

Options:

➤ Ask: 'How does this help?' each time they wander off track.

➤ Restate the purpose of the meeting and point out how their pet topic is irrelevant at this time.

➤ Ask for a reality check about their topic.

➤ If they persist, curtail their speaking time and move on.

➤ If they misuse question time, ask them to ask a relevant question.

➤ If they can't or won't, thank them for their contribution and move on.

The use of the Color Swatch

The use of Color Swatches in small meetings can help to alleviate some of the tricky situations mentioned.

Holding up the appropriate card, participants can let meeting managers know when they have a question, without interrupting proceedings. Dependent upon a participant's characteristics and behavior the meeting manager can decide whether or not to give them 'air time' on this occasion. Being able to indicate when others seem to be going 'off track', allows participants to help with the curtailing the behavior of entertainers, storytellers, axe grinders etc. The use of this card offers an instant reality check when any participant's behavior is perceived by the others to be inappropriate.

Dealing with discomfort

After observing or participating in any of these tricky situations it can be supportive of the people in the meeting to give them an opportunity for reflection and to talk about how they're feeling.

Options:

➤ Taking a moment, pausing for breath, having a moment's silence can allow people to regain their equilibrium.

➤ When this is followed by a Check-In, people can share with one another how they're feeling as a result of the experience.

Having expressed these feelings the group may be able to let them go in order to better concentrate and move on.

Many of these tricky situations are most likely to occur in strictly chaired meetings or those in which the participants feel controlled. These difficulties may be avoided in facilitated meetings because the structure and the processes employed give participants more ownership of their meeting. Meetings are often most effective when designed to encourage equality in discussion and the free flow of information and ideas. This way, participants can be fully engaged with one another in an open, respectful and co-operative manner.

Unfinished agendas

Overwhelm arising from being faced with too many agenda items or frustration in dealing with irrelevant topics can derail a meeting. Doggedly plodding through items without due consideration to appropriate timing can cause meetings to overrun and for agendas to remain unfinished.

Options:

> - Be realistic about the number of items that can be properly and comfortably dealt with during the time available.

> - Before formal meetings, send out the agenda in plenty of time for attendees to be aware of what they will be covering and to gather any information or materials they will be required to bring to the meeting.

> - At the same time send out any extra necessary reading material so that attendees can be acquainted with this rather than using time during the meeting to get up to speed.

> - Create a Visible Agenda on a flip chart or white board. This keeps the agenda in full view and allows the participants to keep track of the progress of the meeting more easily than when the agenda is on individual sheets of paper for each participant. This method helps the whole group to take some responsibility for the progress of the meeting.

> - Working with the participants, create an Open Agenda on a flip chart or whiteboard to ensure that items have real relevance for them and a greater potential for achieving the intended outcomes. Mutual ownership of the agenda can increase commitment to progressing it to completion and avoid the discord between participants and meeting managers that can arise from participants feeling controlled.

> - Cross out items as they are completed. This can provide a sense of achievement, while reminding participants of what is still left to be handled.

Lingerers

At the end of meetings some people may be reluctant to leave. There can be a number of reasons for this. They could feel energized by the proceedings. They may want to continue the discussion with one or more members of the group. They may want to express ideas that have just occurred to them or which they felt unable to articulate during the meeting. They may just not want to go home.

Options:

> - Create a social time, perhaps with some refreshment, to take place after the meeting.

- Perhaps these conversations can continue while you tidy away the meeting paraphernalia and reset the room as it was before you arrived.
- If the meeting room needs to be closed up or someone is waiting to lock up, clearly and respectfully point this out to people.
- Encourage those who are still animated to carry on their conversations elsewhere.
- Bring the awareness of these ongoing conversations into the debriefing of the meeting to consider if there was more that could have been done to facilitate these during the meeting time.

If people want to talk to you as meeting manager or to offer ideas and suggestions after the meeting you have a number of options.
- You can listen to them there and then.
- You can arrange a time when it will be more convenient to do so.
- You can gently remind those people that the processes during the meeting and the feedback session at the end were intended to create opportunities for them to express their views.
- Invite them to participate in the debriefing, if appropriate.
- Ask them to bring their thoughts and ideas to the next meeting.

Lonely or unhappy people might want to extend the time in which they are able to be with people.
- Seek their help in tidying up the room.
- Give them something to do in preparation for the next meeting.
- Bring your awareness of their situation into the debriefing process to consider ways in which they can become more involved in the future.
- Balance efficiency with compassion.

If there is no need at all for you to take any action about these lingering people, then leave them to enjoy being with one another.

 Things to remember:
- Usually, the participants in meetings/events are adults and deserve to be treated as such.
- All behavior is communication.
- Inappropriate behavior is usually based upon fear, uncertainty or lack of experience.
- We all have needs that we wish to have met.
- We all have off days.
- We can all do better with a little compassionate support.

5

READYMADE MEETING AND EVENT DESIGNS

Obviously, many meetings and events will need to be specifically designed to fit the circumstances, the participants and the intended outcomes. However, in some cases much of the designing of a meeting might have already been done. A range of readymade designs for meetings and events exist that could be used for a variety of purposes. Most of these formulas could be facilitated as complete meetings or they might be used as significant processes in large events.

People new to facilitation might find it useful to try out their skills and gain confidence in their abilities by facilitating events based upon these readymade meeting designs before launching into designing their own.

One of the most useful meeting/event designs for initiating community action is Action Search.

Action Search

Action Search is a process designed to support organizations, groups or sections of the community to come together to consider various aspects of an issue, to create a common vision for the future regarding an issue or to initiate projects that could ensure that future.

Large numbers of people can participate. They are divided into small stakeholder groups to search for common ground amongst themselves regarding wishes for the future that are appropriate for their collective needs. This Common Ground can then form the basis for identifying actions to be taken and projects to be created. If required, the whole gathering can then seek to combine these areas of Common Ground into a statement of vision or purpose to which those present can feel aligned.

Although the steps described below form the basis of an Action Search they are not set in stone. This design can be adapted to suit the needs of specific groups.

Planning an Action Search event

Planning an Action Search takes time, effort and resources. To guarantee a successful and rewarding outcome, some positive answers to the following questions are essential.

Is an action search appropriate?
Factors in deciding whether or not an Action Search is appropriate are:
a. Does the participating group have an existing structure that can convert the discovered Common Ground and vision into meaningful projects?
b. If not, can such a structure be created?
c. Does the group have the commitment and willingness to spend the time working on its vision for the future?
d. If this is in an organization, is it possible to bring together a wide enough group of stakeholders within it to ensure that the people who control the organization's resources and develop its policies will support the exercise and its outcomes?
e. Is it possible to bring together a wide enough group of stakeholder representatives if an Action Search is to be used in community situations such as community planning?
f. If this is a public gathering, is it possible to bring together a wide enough group of appropriate stakeholders to make the event productive and the results meaningful?

If there is any real doubt about any of these, then a wiser strategy may be to apply other meeting methods and processes in the organization's, group's, or community's usual program of meetings. The use of these methods could help people to develop the capacities and attitudes that are required to actively participate in and gain the full benefits from an Action Search.

Naming the event
Care ought to be taken when naming an Action Search event in order to attract the most appropriate attendees. Titles that describe the intended

beneficial outcome are often most effective. For public gatherings that could be something like: 'Creating Co-operative Community'. In organizations it might be: 'Ensuring Mutual Efficiency'. Sometimes naming the type of event with a strap-line containing the issue to be explored can be useful, such as: Community Forum - Youth Matters.

Who could attend?
➢ Anyone who has a stake in the outcome of the Action Search.
➢ Anyone who will want to be involved in any resulting projects.
➢ Anyone who will be affected by those projects.
(In large gatherings representatives of these people might be delegated)

Who ought to be there?
a. In large organizations or community gatherings representatives of stakeholder groups need to be identified and invited to the gathering.
b. If the resulting projects may require a variety of resources then attendance by representatives from the relevant sources of these resources might be essential.

Initial Action Search Steps
A pilot group is formed to identify the issue upon which the Action Search is to be based. This group identifies the appropriate stakeholders, puts together a group of Action Search facilitators, books the venue and sets the date, issues the invitations to the event, puts out any necessary publicity and organizes the support systems such as catering, crèche facilities, transport and perhaps accommodation for out of town visitors.

> Some effort may need to be made to encourage some of the necessary stakeholder representatives to attend. Especially at community events when people will be giving their time freely for the common good.

Creating Home Groups
Participants are arranged into home groups of 4 to 10 people depending on the numbers expected, the stakeholder interests and the outcome desired. These home groups are most often comprised of stakeholder representatives in their areas of similar interest. In an organization these could be departments or divisions. In communities these could be areas such as finance, transport, families, education etc. These specific stakeholder groups will need to be pre-arranged to ensure the appropriate groupings are in place.

In an Action Search where the participants do not represent stakeholder groups then the subject or aspect of the topic that each home group will consider can be stated on the registration form that is sent out prior to the day. To ensure that each group will have appropriate numbers, people can register their topics of interests in order of preference. As the forms are returned participants can be allocated to a group either through appropriateness or on a first come basis. As people arrive they are informed of their home group.

In some community situations people's interests or concerns may not be apparent. In this case perhaps only some vital participants may need to commit to the event and other people can just turn up. If the publicity has been effective, the right people will be there.

Another method for grouping people is to place a sign indicating the subject to be considered on each table. Participants can sort themselves into home groups by sitting at the table of their choice.

If some tables have too many people a request can be made for some of them to move to tables where there are too few. If some people are reluctant to do so that group could be divided into groups of manageable numbers to consider different aspects of that topic. If some tables have too few people for meaningful discussion, these people could be asked to join other tables that are not overwhelmed with participants.

If a table has no takers this could indicate an obvious lack of interest in that topic. This may be because the subject has little bearing on the event or it may point to lack of awareness or even to some avoidance. Such subjects can turn out to be like an elephant in the room that everyone knows is there and yet nobody wants to acknowledge. These subjects can be stumbling blocks to success and may even lead to some level of failure. Although it may not be appropriate to deal with these during the event, such topics may need to be acknowledged or addressed at some time to prevent them from impeding progress towards an envisioned better future.

Room set up

The room is set up with chairs around tables. Each table can have a variety of ways for people to record their thoughts: flipchart and paper, strips of butcher's paper, small sheets of paper, post-it notes, pens, pencils and a variety of colored markers.

A table is placed at the front of the room for the facilitator or facilitating team.

The walls and perhaps even some of the windows are made ready to receive sheets of information created by each group. Pins, tape, white or blue tack or other suitable adhering items need to be on hand.

Upon arrival

Colored dots or a similar device is used at registration to allocate people to their home group tables, which are clearly labeled.

The purpose of the event and object of the exercise is clearly stated in the welcoming remarks by the convener of the event or the lead facilitator. The facilitator describes the Action Search process in sufficient detail for everyone to fully understand what he or she is supposed to do. Questions are answered and points clarified.

The process

There are twelve steps to this process.

Step one

Each home group now appoints a person to each of the following roles: Table Facilitator, Recorder and Time-keeper.

Step two

Everyone in each group introduces themselves to each other in a Go-Round. They state their name, even if it is on their nametag and the stake holding group they represent, if appropriate. Other information they give could be the reason they have attended, what they hope to get out of the day and any further relevant information they want the group to know about. One or two minutes per person ought to be allowed for these introductions, dependent upon the number of people at each table. The time-keeper is responsible for timing this and making sure that this process is complete by the time of the next step.

Step three

Each person now works by himself or herself to imagine their vision for the project/community/project, etc. in a future year... 2030 for example.

a. They are to consider this from the perspective of their particular interest and from their personal point of view.

b. They are to imagine themselves being the same age then as they are now.

c. They are to make this an optimistic vision – what they would like to see, not what they fear may happen.

d. They are to be encouraged to think expansively and not to allow their vision to be restricted by any limiting factors.

e. They are to think broadly while noting any detail that comes to mind.

f. They are to take charge in visioning and making their future ideal just right for themselves and those they represent.

As this is a vital component of the day, plenty of time ought to be allowed for this process.

Step four

In a Go-Round managed by the Table Facilitator, the group listens attentively to each person describing their vision of the future. The major points are recorded on large sheets of paper. When everybody has had their turn there is another Go-Round for each person to speak briefly about something they found to be positive and interesting during the presentations. Some of these are also recorded.

Step five

Each group now looks for areas of Common Ground in their visions and develops a composite vision for their home group that combines these. An element becomes Common Ground when all or an agreed majority of members of the group want to include it in the composite vision. A synopsis of each of these is listed or mind-mapped on a flip chart and details of each item are also recorded separately on smaller sheets of paper.

It is important to take note of any elements that are rejected. Some work could be carried out on these unresolved issues - those elements that are not agreed to be Common Ground, if time permits. Perhaps new agreements for Common Ground can be reached if wording is changed a little. Disagreements might be overcome when the sentence: 'could agree to it if...' is completed. Unresolved items could be worked through in this way, shifting any newly resolved issues over to Common Ground.

Step six

Each group then creates a presentation to show the whole gathering the vision for the future from their group's perspective. They can do this in any number of ways:

> Through a verbal presentation by one person or the entire group.
> Writing and performing a song, a poem or a mock-up of a video or a radio or TV show.
> Taking people on a journey through visualization.
> Using any mixture of creative styles in a presentation.

Step seven

Each group presents their creation to the whole gathering.

Step eight

Each home group makes a display on the wall. They post up their flip charts showing their vision for the future and the smaller sheets each showing items of unresolved issues.

Step nine

The whole gathering then takes a decent amount of time to study the visions of the other groups. This can be effectively done during the final break.

Step ten

The whole gathering comes together to share thoughts on these displayed sheets and to explore options of utilizing these ideas. This is vital as it allows each group to see one another's visions and have an understanding of how these might be mutually supportive. Connections between visions from the groups could be made; proposals might be combined or clustered and Common Ground within these ideas might be found

Step eleven

The items in each cluster or in each group's Common Ground now form action briefs. Action Groups are set up to explore the elements of the action briefs and to find ways to convert them into projects and actions. This is the main objective of the event. This is what will turn wishes, dreams and visions into the reality of action and practical projects.

People are invited to participate in one of these groups. This is not restricted to the original stakeholder group members. Some definite projects may already have become clear. If so, groups could be created to bring these to fruition.

The Action Groups use the time remaining in the event to formulate some of their strategies, agree the date of their first meeting and allot tasks to each person involved to be completed by that date. These tasks might include researching information, recruiting useful members to the group and informing those who need to know of the intentions of the group.

Unresolved issues that have not become part of an action brief could be considered or researched by their proposers or others and the findings offered to an appropriate Action Group, or in a follow-up meeting or another future gathering.

Step twelve

A closing Go-Round in the new Action Groups which includes such things as something participants have learned, enjoyed, committed to, etc.

The Facilitator or Convener wraps up the event. In their closing remarks they sum up the results of the day, clarify what steps will next be taken by whom and by when, announce the dates and venues of meetings of the Action Groups and any follow-up meeting to be held in the future at which progress will be reported by these groups.

Appreciation is given to the pilot group and those volunteers who have put effort into making the event possible. Appreciation is given to the participants for their effort, their creativity and their willingness. This last part is especially important if the gathering has been a community event where people have given their time freely.

The event is brought to a close.

A process similar to Action Search is facilitated on the third day of Future Search, a powerfully effective three-day event for large groups of people to initiate change and co-create the future within their organization or community. People interested in facilitating these events could search on-line for organizations that offer training in this methodology.

There's more

Action Search, World Café Conversations and Open Space Technology are only some of the meeting designs that have been created by experienced people dedicated to encouraging cooperative, inclusive and enjoyable meetings and events. For many years these designs have been widely used in a variety of situations around the world.

Detailed descriptions and instructions for these and many more readymade meeting designs are in the book: EFFORTLESS FACILITATION, in the YOU MAKE THE DIFFERENCE series.

This book contains a great deal of information on the planning and facilitating of a variety of types of meetings and events. It is packed with tools, tips, suggestions, insights and methods for developing or improving skills and achieving excellence in facilitation. Anyone keen to expand their skills in facilitation and further improve the quality of their work might find this book interesting and useful.

This is available in paperback and Kindle eBook from Amazon and accessible through our website: www.youmakethedifference.net

6

EFFECTIVE PARTICIPATION

No matter how well intentioned, well planned, or well managed a meeting is it would be pointless if people didn't participate when they got there.

Whether a meeting is called to discuss the playgroup Christmas party or an event to plan the future development of a significant project, the outcomes will be largely the responsibility of the participants.

People could make the difference to your meetings and events by developing some of the skills and attitudes required for becoming effective participants.

Participants could be provided with the following guidelines. Alternatively, as these are in our short Guide to Effective and Enjoyable Meetings, participants could freely download them in PDF and e-book format from our website: www.youmakethedifference.net/free-guides.html

A guide to being an effective participant

Be willing to participate

If you want a meeting to achieve a specific outcome it is no good leaving it up to other people. Be willing to be involved.

Show up

Having decided to participate, do so whole-heartedly. Show up with the whole of you present. Bring your passions, your skills, your information, your experience and your attention.

Be clear about the purpose.

Before the meeting, get clear about its purpose and gather any facts and figures that will assist you in being a productive participant. For formal meetings such as committee or Trustees meetings, the agenda and all relevant reading material ought to be available to all the attendees at least one week prior to the meeting. This is to save time during the meeting and to provide enough time for uncertainties to be clarified and questions to be prepared. If this is not happening in the formal meetings that you attend, request it to be so.

Know Your Own Mind

Before the meeting, work out what you think about the subject as far as you can. Consider what you would like as an outcome. Define your own thoughts and decide what contribution you can make. Knowing your own mind can put you miles ahead of many people who show up 'light headed' to meetings. Many meetings might take only a short time if everybody came with carefully considered ideas or suggestions.

Keep an open mind

Being clear about what you want the meeting to achieve ought not to prevent you from having an open mind to other people's ideas. Their perspective and experience will be different from yours and may provide valuable insights, information and suggestions.

Listen attentively

Knowing what the meeting is attempting to achieve and what you think about it will allow you to listen attentively and with an open mind to what the others have to say. Listen to hear if people are aligned with the same purpose you are. Listen to understand other perspectives. Listen to learn what cross-purposes might need to be straightened out before meaningful discussion can take place.

Attempt to understand what each person wants out of the meeting. If the other participants are ready to work on the same problem, what do they want the solution to be? Are they cemented into their positions, or are they willing to listen to other perspectives?

Through attentive listening you can spot the people who are likely to get in the way of a productive meeting. They are the ones who want to crack jokes, tell stories, pick fights, get their own way, boss people around, be noticed or give up before they start.

Make and Keep Agreements

Timing, behavior and sometimes confidentiality, are areas that ought to be agreed upon. If these agreements are not part of the meetings you attend, ask for them to be made. Having made these agreements it is your responsibility to keep to them. If other participants stray from honoring these agreements, you could support the meeting manager by respectfully bringing everyone's awareness back to the agreements that have been made.

Keep to time

An important aspect of effective meetings is good time-keeping. Poor time-keeping may cause frustration, resentment and unfinished agendas and often results in failure to achieve the full purpose of the meeting. As a participant it is your responsibility to turn up on time and deliver your information and views in a clear and concise manner within the time allotted to you.

Contribute

Attending meetings is pointless unless you are willing to contribute and clearly make your views known. Before the meeting, obtain any facts and figures that are needed and organize them in a way that will make them easy to present efficiently. You can include your ideas and suggestions, your doubts and your hopes. If you've done your homework, know the purpose, and are clear about your own views, your contribution will be comprehensible, concise, and appropriate. Take a genuine interest in other people's ideas and look for ways of combining and refining the good ones.

Keep Your Cool

Be honest about any concerns in a calm manner. Displaying anger and other emotions or being brutally honest may not help to achieve a positive outcome to meetings. The group's purpose ought to be more important than the opinions and concerns of individual participants.

Sometimes your expression of feelings may need to be tempered to the task at hand. It will assist the group for you to speak to everyone calmly and respectfully, even when you do not like a person or deeply disagree with their opinions. There may be times when it shows strength of character to let unfair criticism pass in silence, and to allow obvious small fallacies go unchallenged in the service of group harmony and getting the job done. The sort of withheld feelings that would destroy an intimate relationship could be the saving of an important meeting.

People who have an understanding of Constructive Communication can have a positive influence on the behavior of other participants.

Understand good meeting management

Even if you are a participant with no aspirations to manage meetings, it may help you to understand how meetings can be well managed. By learning the procedures, methods and processes that can improve the quality of meetings, you could gently and respectfully (and possibly privately) acquaint the managers of your meetings with these if you think it would help. This is not about undermining them in anyway. It is about making your contribution to meetings.

There may be opportunities during meetings to suggest some small things that could enhance a discussion or resolve a tricky situation. These can be offered as suggestions or requests: 'I would really like to see the faces of everyone during the meeting. How about making a circle with the chairs so that we can all see each other?' 'I realize that I don't know everybody here, could we just go around the circle/table and introduce ourselves and say why we are here and what we would like to get out of the meeting?' 'I would appreciate having a little time to think about this question.' 'I recently learned the benefits of a Think and Listen process which could be helpful to us.' 'I'm interested in what everybody thinks about this, can we go around the circle/table to hear everyone's opinion?'

Modeling behavior

You can make the difference to the meetings you attend by managing your behavior, making your contributions positive and taking responsibility for the quality of your communication. Through modeling these you could influence others at the meeting to do the same.

Manage your energy

Some topics may require a lot of concentration. However, that ought not to be debilitating. Look after yourself. Ask for breaks when you need them. You will probably be speaking up for many other people too. Stand up and stretch. Move around. Get some fresh air. Do whatever you need to do to stay alert and fully present and engaged.

Remain positive

Your anticipation of a bountiful harvest of ideas will encourage them to emerge. Your positive expectation of a beneficial outcome will help to achieve that. The enthusiasm that brought you to the meeting in the first place is what could sustain your positive attitude.

Enjoy yourself

Even though some meetings might be dealing with serious and important issues, this is no reason for them to be miserable affairs. Appreciate being with like-minded people, especially if the meetings you attend are within projects through which you intend to make some positive difference.

Enjoy using your intellect and sharing your experience and expertise. Use appropriate humor within good-natured discussions. Have fun!

 Things worth remembering as a participant

About yourself:
  a.   You can only do your best.
  b.   You have a right to your opinions and beliefs, no matter how irrational they may seem to other people.
  c.   You can take responsibility for your communication and your behavior in meetings.
  d.   You can be supportive to other participants and to the meeting managers.
  e.   You can positively make the difference to the meetings you attend.

About your meeting managers:
  a.   They will be doing their best.
  b.   Some are more skilled than others.
  c.   Some might never have expected to be required to manage meetings.
  d.   They have been willing to step up to manage the meeting.
  e.   Together you can make meetings enjoyable and effective.

In conclusion

Effectively managed meetings can save enormous amounts of time, effort and money for the groups, organizations or projects that they are intended to support. The participants in enjoyable, skillfully and mindfully managed meetings and events are likely to leave them feeling satisfied that their time has been well spent.

Managing those meetings successfully to create the desired outcomes can be immensely rewarding. Hopefully, this book will have provided you with some information, methods, skills, tools and insights to make a positive and significant difference to every meeting you manage.

MORE YOU MAKE THE DIFFERENCE BOOKS

Ripples created by our actions inevitably make some difference in the world. These books are intended to encourage and help people who want to make a positive difference to their lives and to the world around them.

YOU MAKE THE DIFFERENCE
Through
EFFORTLESS FACILITATION

This book is packed with suggestions for planning and designing meetings and events, useful methods and tips for facilitation, empowering and productive processes and a variety of ready-made meeting designs to fit many situations. The implementation of these will guarantee inexperienced facilitators becoming skillful and experienced facilitators becoming even more accomplished – effortlessly!

YOU MAKE THE DIFFERENCE
Through
ENJOYABLE & VALUABLE
VOLUNTEERING

This book contains simple and exciting methods for people to explore what skills and experience they could volunteer, where and how they can easily make their valuable contribution, how to look after themselves while effectively helping others and the many enjoyable ways in which volunteering will enrich their own lives.

YOU MAKE THE DIFFERENCE
Through
EMPOWERING VOLUNTEER MANAGMENT

This book contains many suggestions for finding, recruiting, supporting, empowering, managing and keeping volunteers. Following these guidelines and using the insights into what volunteers need to be efficient, effective, valuable and fulfilled in their roles, will guarantee empowered volunteers.

YOU MAKE THE DIFFERENCE
Through
SUCCESSFUL
GROUPS & PROJECTS

This book offers insights into how groups work and why they sometimes fail, successful startup and maintenance of projects that achieve the purpose and objectives, methods for attracting and keeping appropriate members and volunteers. The adoption and implementation of the suggested attitudes, the strategies for obtaining resources, the efficient use of time, money, skills and effort, and the respectful, cooperative ways people can enjoy working together will guarantee success of any group or project.

YOU MAKE THE DIFFERENCE
Through
´ INSPIRING COMMUNITY
SUSTAINABILITY

The answer to many of the difficulties facing society is creating a greater sense of community. This book is filled with information and insights, developed through decades of research and experience, on the elements essential for achieving sustainability in any form of community. Utilizing this information, adopting the suggested attitudes, and implementing the recommended systems and processes will guarantee greater sustainability in communities, whether they are rural or urban, traditional or intentional, Transition Towns or Ecovillages.

YOU MAKE THE DIFFERENCE
Through
SMART TALKING

Each time we open our mouths to speak we will inevitably have an impact upon those to whom we are talking. This book aims to show the consequences of having a negative impact and offers insightful suggestions for creating a positive effect. Following these guidelines and the suggested attitudes, skills and tools that can relieve stress, enhance relationships and improve communication in so many areas of life will guarantee anyone becoming a Smart Talker.

YOU MAKE THE DIFFERENCE
Through
SMART LISTENING

Each of us will inevitably have an impact upon the individuals to whom we listen that is either positive and beneficial or negative and potentially damaging to individuals and society. Implementing the attitudes, listening skills, tools and techniques suggested in this book will guarantee a positive effect that will greatly improve personal and working relationships, reduce conflict, enhance many areas of life and be supportive to people's confidence and self-esteem.

YOU MAKE THE DIFFERENCE
Through
SMART TALKING
& LISTENING TO CHILDREN

From the moment children are born they are learning to become the adults who will manage the future. What kind of future might adults be influencing through the way they talk and listen to children? This book is crammed with skills, tools, insights and suggestions on how adults can be supportive through their communication to the development of youngsters and contribute towards a safe, sustainable future in the hands of well adjusted, capable, empowered, responsible and caring people.

ABOUT
YOU MAKE THE DIFFERENCE

Tim and Kay Kay, the two generations of cultural creatives, who founded YOU MAKE THE DIFFERENCE, believe that it is now essential for people to behave supportively with another, to become more engaged in their local community and to cooperate and work collaborate together for a sustainable future. The books and website are intended to encourage and support people to achieve the positive difference they wish to make in their lives and in the world around them.

To help with this, Kay Kay, the author, offers decades of experience gained in a variety of professions and cultures, and shares her practical philosophy, knowledge, skills and insights into beneficial ways of behaving, working and communicating with one another and contributing to society.

Tim, as collaborator, book designer, publisher and Webmaster, brings his creativity as an artist and writer, his in-depth knowledge of Buddhist philosophy and the skills and considerable experience gained through living, working and studying in many countries.

All the YOU MAKE THE DIFFERENCE books are intended to be enjoyable to read and easy to use - by everyone. The wealth of information is concisely written to be of benefit to professionals wishing to upgrade their skills; busy people working to make a difference in their communities and at the grassroots of their societies, and people from different cultures, especially those from the developing world, for whom English may be a 2nd or even 3rd language.

On the website: www.youmakethedifference.net there is more background information; GUIDES on a variety of interesting and useful subjects that are FREE to download and the opportunity for people to become part of the Global YOU MAKE THE DIFFERENCE network.

"We each make a difference in the world every moment through our words, actions and behavior, whether we are aware of it or not. The trick to being a smart human being is to choose to make a positive difference."

Kay Kay